A GUIDE TO MUSIC AROUND THE WORLD

P. Dunbar-Hall

G. Hodge

S

Science Press

for Julian and Hannah

Science Press
Fitzroy and Chapel Streets
Marrickville NSW 2204
Tel. (02) 516 1122 Fax. (02) 550 1915
©Science Press 1991

First published 1991

National Library of Australia
Cataloguing-in-Publication data

Dunbar-Hall, P. (Peter).
    A guide to music around the world.

    Bibliography.
    Includes index.
    ISBN 0 85583 181 2.

    1. Ethnomusicology. I. Hodge, G. (Glenda). II. Title.

780.89

Front Cover Photographs
A Tutsi war dance, Rwanda
Photograph: Michael Calnan, World Expeditions, Sydney

Balinese dancers
Photograph: Garuda Indonesia

Korean court musicians
Photograph: The Korea National Tourism Corporation

Back Cover Photograph
A Peruvian flute player
Photograph: Luis Cuadros, Panorama Tours, Sydney

Text design by Lesley Brown
Cover design by Joan McGirr
Maps by Valda R. Brook

Set in 11/12pt. Palacio
Printed in Singapore.

Typeset by
Authotype Photosetters Pty. Ltd. Sydney.

Contents

1
The Study of
MUSIC
from Other
Cultures

Balkan musicians play the drum and *zurna*

Introduction

The aim of this book is to introduce you to music from a number of different countries. The music that will be discussed is often referred to as folk music, though definitions of this term are varied. What all the music has in common is that it was orally transmitted — in other words, it was not composed and notated by a composer but was passed on from one person to the next 'by ear'. We say 'was' because now it is possible to buy collections of music that have been transcribed and printed, and the traditional method of learning music is becoming less common.

There are a number of different names for this area of study: ethnomusicology, comparative musicology, or musical ethnography. There is no common agreement over which term should be used but they all refer to the study of music of an oral tradition that exists apart from European art music. This music includes tribal music (e.g. Koori music of the rural Australian Aborigines), folk music (e.g. that played and sung in a Greek village), and music of developed cultures that is not written down (e.g. some Asian music).

Whatever the term used for this study, the goal is to find out about the music by looking at examples of it, both recorded and notated, and by playing it. To help you do this we have focused on a number of features: the uses of distinctive scales, rhythmic practices, form, the functions of musical examples, and the instruments used by specific countries. Remember, the idea is to study the music and actively learn how it uses musical elements, not to learn about it just by reading. For this reason each country studied includes pieces of music to be played, sung, and analysed. There is also an accompanying tape of examples to introduce you to some of the sounds and instruments of these countries. As well, you should listen to as much music from these countries as you can — these days, the amount of recorded material available and the broadcasting of music from different cultures on both radio and television will help to make this easy for you.

Notation

Notation of the music presents its own problems. Not all music can be notated on a five line stave using the rhythmic notation of Western music. Other countries have their own systems of notation, some of which act as memory devices rather than complete representations of a piece of music. For example, some *gamelan* music in Java is written down as a series of numbers referring to the notes to be played on an instrument, but the rhythm is not shown as this depends on the players knowing how their part fits together with the other players. This knowledge can only be gained through practical experience: playing the piece with the other musicians. *Gamelan* music provides a good example of how the process known as 'oral tradition' works because the music is learned and passed on from one person to the next by playing it and remembering it.

Instruments

Another problem area in this subject is the description and classification of musical instruments. In this book we will use two methods: the Sachs–Hornbostel system and analogous description.

Indian trumpets

The Sachs–Hornbostel system

The Sachs–Hornbostel system of classification of musical instruments was devised in 1914 by Curt Sachs and Erich Hornbostel. It systematises more than three hundred individual types of instruments into four main classes: idiophones (80), membranophones (63), chordophones (70), and aerophones (122). The main members of each class are given in the following list.

Membranophones

These are instruments which have skins as their main sounding source, and a resonating body which can be of any shape or material. Drums are included in this category.

Idiophones

In this classification are instruments — such as rattles, shakers, gongs and rasps — that make their sound 'by themselves'. Body percussion such as hand clapping is included here.

Chordophones

These instruments produce their sounds by vibrating strings, either plucked, strummed, bowed, or hit. Usually the sound is amplified by the hollow body of the instrument. Included in this group are the violin, *rebab*, guitar and *santur*.

Aerophones

Aerophones are instruments that are blown, including those with reeds, those that work from the buzzing of the player's lips, and whistle instruments. These can be made from a variety of materials such as wood, metal, bone and clay. This group includes flutes and trumpets.

Sometimes instruments can belong to more than one classification, for instance a drum that also has rattles attached.

A Chinese drum dance

Analogous description

In this method, instruments are described according to their common features. For example, an Indonesian *rebab* (a chordophone in the Sachs–Hornbostel system) can be described as a two-stringed fiddle, implying a string instrument with two strings, played by a bow. In this case the word 'fiddle' is an accepted term for an instrument type of which the Western violin is also an example.

There is an accepted group of analogous terms for describing instrument types which has been used throughout the book. Where they are used you will see them referred to as '. . . – type' or 'like a . . .'. This means that an instrument has the same general characteristics as the nominated type.

- Lute   stringed instrument with a body and neck, the strings usually being plucked
- Zither   stringed instrument in which the strings are horizontal above the sounding board and are either hit with small hammers or sticks or plucked by the fingers or plectra
- Dulcimer   stringed instrument in which the strings are horizontal above the sounding board and are plucked by the fingers or plectra in or on the fingers
- Harp   stringed instrument where the strings are at an angle to the sounding board
- Fiddle   a bowed, stringed instrument
- Flute   a blown instrument where the sound is produced by nothing other than the player's breath
- Oboe   a blown instrument in which the sound is made by two reeds
- Trumpet   a blown instrument where the sound originates with the buzzing of the player's lips
- Mouth Organ   a set of blown reed pipes

Sacred flutes, Papua New Guinea

Four-stringed harps, Chad

In this book we use both the Sach–Hornbostel classification system because it is the conventional scientific way to discuss instruments, and analogous description because this method helps students identify instruments by reference to those they already know.

One of the things you will notice as you work through this book is that some instruments appear in a number of countries, sometimes with the same or a similar name. Some examples are the Chinese *sheng* and the Japanese *sho*, the Turkish *zurna* or *surnay* and the Chinese and Vietnamese *sona*.

The process of borrowing between cultures can be particularly significant when one country has been colonised by another. In some cases, the influence of the colonising country is so strong that aspects of its music are fully incorporated into the traditional music of the colonised country. As a result the traditional music of the country is changed. We see an example of this in the music of the Pacific Islands where European instruments and styles are an accepted part of the traditional music. This process is known as 'acculturation'.

The music we have selected for study comes from five large geographical areas: Asia (India, Indonesia, Vietnam, China, Korea and Japan); South America (the Andean area and Brazil) and the Caribbean; the eastern Mediterranean (Yugoslavia, Greece, Turkey and Iran); the Pacific region (Papua New Guinea, Australian Aborigines, New Zealand Maoris, Fiji, Tonga and Hawaii); and Africa.

After you have been right through the book, the final section contains follow-up activities related to the music you have studied. There are assignments in which you find examples of music by composers of art music that have been influenced by 'folk music', and the chance for you to select other countries to study for yourself. As well there are worksheets to be used when you listen to recorded examples to help you analyse the music. Throughout the book there are listening exercises and pieces to perform. Song lyrics are given in their original languages with translations for most songs included at the end of the book.

Whichever countries you choose to study, remember that we are learning about the music by learning the music — that is, by performing it and noticing how it uses the elements of music.

Peruvian musicians and dancers

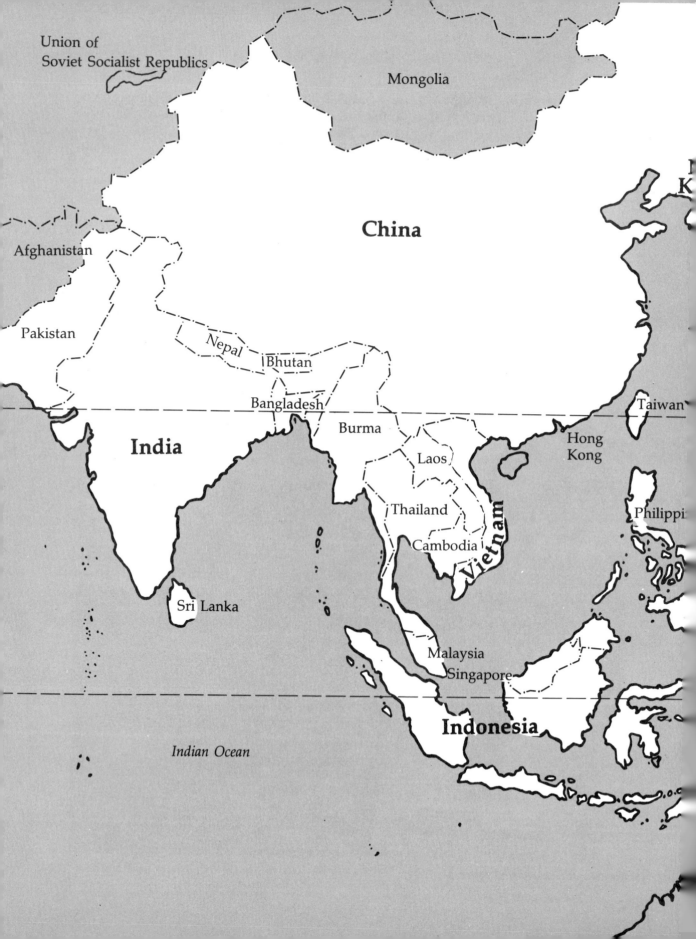

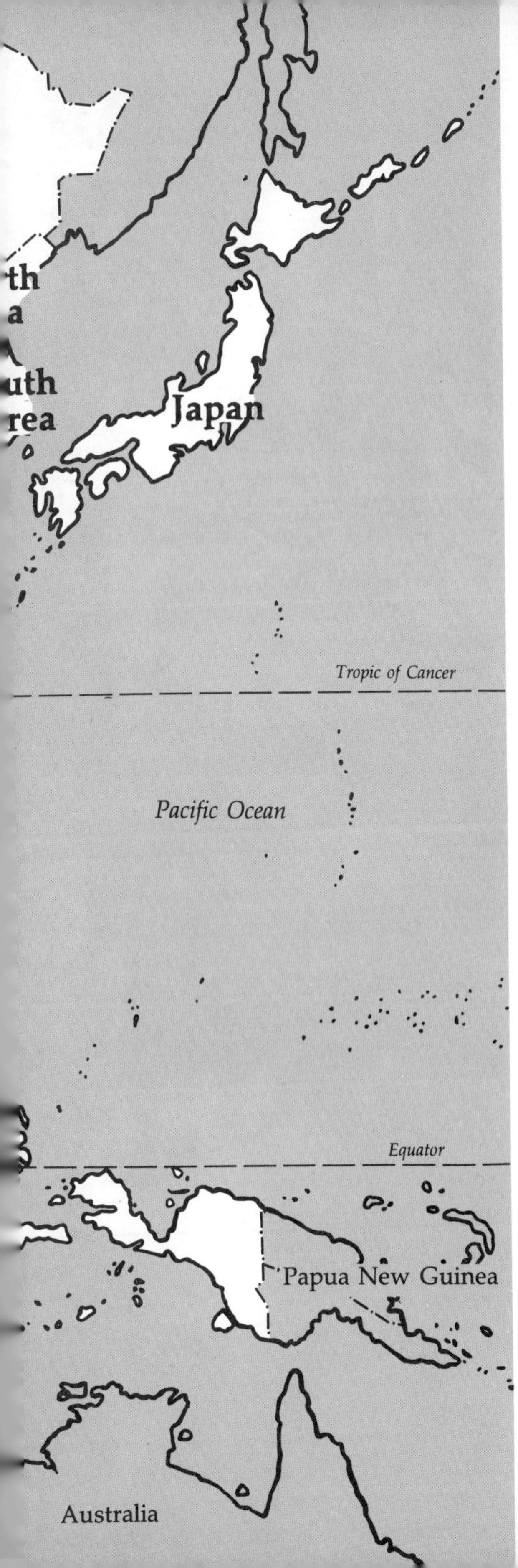

2
ASIA

Japan

th
a
uth
rea

Tropic of Cancer

Pacific Ocean

Equator

Papua New Guinea

Australia

China

Chinese musical history goes back many thousands of years. Written references to Chinese music were made 3000 years ago and for 2000 years before that legends and folk stories about the beginnings of music were told. The Chinese symbol for the word music (*yue*) is 2300 years old.

Ancient China was an agricultural society and its sorcerer-priests of long ago played an important social and religious role as they danced and sang for rain, defence from enemies and protection from the elements. The rulers of China, the emperors, maintained the importance of music not only for entertainment but also for social and political reasons.

Early Chinese dynasties were slave societies and slaves were often trained as professional musicians and dancers. These musicians and their instruments — clay ocarinas, whistles and flutes of bamboo, stone chimes and drums — were often buried alive with their masters.

Historians have categorised the development of Chinese music into four periods:

Formative Period (3000 BC– 400 AD)

Chinese music history is said to have begun when the Emperor Huang Ti sent his court musician, Ling Lun, to the western mountains of China where he was inspired by the three and four note songs of birds. These became the basis of the pentatonic scale. Ling Lun also returned with bamboo to make instruments. Chinese (and Asian music in general) has maintained close links with nature ever since.

The philosopher Confucius (*c* 550–478 BC) saw music as a way of achieving universal harmony. Music that was 'virtuous' and pure (*ya*) was to be prized over the vulgar folk music (*su*) of the people. Court music became stylised and ritualised, remaining unchanged for centuries, while folk music developed into a rich and exciting musical style based on story-telling still popular today. Many of the folk tunes were adopted by the court and so became acceptable 'classical' pieces. Large court orchestras made up of string, wind and percussion instruments often contained more than two hundred performers.

China expanded its borders and was, in turn, invaded by neighbouring countries throughout this time. Instruments such as the *pipa* with songs and musical styles from India and Central Asia were adopted by the Chinese.

International Period (400 – 900 AD)

During this period, invasion and war meant that Chinese culture was further influenced by other nearby countries, mainly Islamic ones such as India, Persia and Turkestan. Distinctive regional music styles also developed within China.

National Period (900 –1900 AD)

Musical styles such as Chinese opera were standardised.

World Music Period (1900 AD –)

Though the first European music came to China with the Jesuit missionaries in the 1600s, Western technology, form and musical styles have only become important this century. Western instrumentation, scales and sounds are widespread in China today.

◁ A group of folk musicians accompany a dancer on string and wind instruments

A bronze drum performance with the accompaniment of a large wooden drum and trumpets

From around 3000 BC, the time of Emperor Huang Ti, Chinese music has been based on the five note or pentatonic scale, though scales of six (hexatonic) and seven (heptatonic) notes are also very old (more than two thousand years). The five notes of the pentatonic scale can be in any of its five modes and these are varied in performance by microtonal shadings and ornamentation:

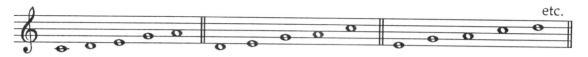

'Hua Ku Ko' is an example of a pentatonic song. Notice the use of crushed notes and the sedentary rhythm:

Hua Ku Ko (verses 2 and 3)

2. (Nü-jén)
   Wo ming k'u, Chen ming k'u!
   Yi sheng yi shih chia pucho hao chang fu.
   Jen chia chang fu tso kuan tso fu,
   Wo chia chang fu tan hui ta hua ku.
   Ta ta hua ku. Ai-ya-ai-hu-ya.
      Drr-lang-dang-p'iao-yi-p'iao,etc.

3. (Nán-jén)
   Wo ming po, Chen ming po!
   Yi sheng yi shih ch'ii pucho hao loa p'o.
   Jen chia lao p'o hsiu hua yu hsiu to,
   Wo chia lao p'o yi shuang ta hua chio.
   Liang la liang liang yi ch'ih to. Ai-ya-ai-hu-ya.
      Drrr-lang-dang-p'iao-yi-p'iao, etc.

Hua Ku Ko

Chinese Folk Song

Chinese music, like Asian music in general, does not make use of harmony as we know it. Chinese music is said to be heterophonic, which means that there are several different parts or instrumental lines but they all play the same melody, each developing or ornamenting it independently as they progress. Occasionally, a melodic line can be doubled an octave lower, or a fourth or fifth higher (giving the characteristic Asian sound), but this is rare and found only in formal court or ritual music.

China was one of the first civilisations to develop a written language and as music was highly regarded, it is natural that a form of musical notation was devised. In fact there are several methods of notation. Most have to do with instructions on how to play instruments or are memory aids. Melodies themselves were generally learnt by rote from a master musician or teacher. Rhythms were not notated, which left the performer free to improvise. In Chinese music, the sound of the performance and the emotions that it stirs in the listener is more prized than sheer virtuosity. This also applies to the music of other countries, such as Korea and Japan, which were influenced by Chinese music.

At the turn of this century, a system of notation based on the tonic sol-fa was introduced. The number 1 stands for doh, 2 for re and so on:

doh	re	mi	fa	soh	lah	te	doh
1	2	3	4	5	6	7	i

0 denotes a rest. Dots above or below a number indicate that the note is to be played an octave higher or lower. Rhythms are given by the presence of lines below the number. Crotchets are played if no line is present. A single line indicates a quaver and double lines indicate semiquavers. Dashes after the note extend the note's value as shown:

Try to write out the missing notes under the notation given:

From: 'Song of Happiness'

Here is a piece of music for you to perform. The 'Song of Happiness' is written in modern Chinese notation. Suggested instruments are given.

歡樂歌
Song of Happiness

江南絲竹

1. recorder/flute (*ti*); 2. melodica (*sheng*); 3. mandolin (*liuyeqin*); 4. lute (*pipa*); 5. banjo (*sanxian*); 6. guitar (*ruan*); 7. dulcimer (*yangqin*); 8. violin (*erhu*); 9. percussion (*cymbals, gongs, bells, woodblocks*)

Instruments

While Western or European instruments were made to imitate the human voice, the music of Asia and its instruments attempt to imitate the sounds of nature. The instruments are made out of the eight elemental families, according to Confucian doctrine (though most instruments are a combination of materials):

chin: metal
shih: stone
t'u: earth or clay
ke: hide or leather
szu: silk
mu: wood
pao: gourd
chu: bamboo

A girl dances as she plays a three-stringed lute

The timbre or quality of sound that an instrument or group of instruments makes is very important in Chinese music. The finest sounds are described as having the 'quality of gold and jade'.

Many instruments are very old, dating back thousands of years. Some examples are bells, sonorous stones or stone chimes (lithophones), drums, ocarinas, mouth organs, pan pipes and zithers. The *qin* (*ch'in*), a zither, dates back more than two thousand years. The *di* (*ti*) and *xiao* (*hsiao*), which are flutes, are also extremely old.

Throughout China's history, new instruments have been introduced through trade, wars and invasions. These include the *pipa* (a lute), bamboo oboes like the Turkish *surnay* (known as the *sona* in China) and the Persian harp or *cank*, which became the *k'ung hou* or *can hou*. Over the last thousand years, these instruments have been 'Sinocised' (integrated into Chinese culture) and are now considered Chinese.

Several instruments which are used in Chinese music are:

String instruments

- *Qin* (*ch'in*): a zither consisting of seven silk strings tuned to the pentatonic scale and stretched over a wooden soundboard 120 cm long. Along the length of the soundboard are inlaid thirteen ivory studs to mark the fret positions. It is played as a solo instrument or to accompany singing. This instrument was first known over two thousand years ago and it was traditionally played out of doors, 'in tune with nature', by a performer kneeling on the ground in front of it. The right hand plucked the strings near the bridge, while the left hand stopped or plucked the strings creating ornamentation with slides and vibratos. There are several zithers varying in numbers of strings but generally of similar shape. Similar instruments to the Chinese *qin* are found in Japan (the *koto*) and Korea (the *kum*).

- *Pipa*: a four-stringed lute with a pear-shaped body. It came to China from Central Asia around fifteen hundred years ago but is now considered a Chinese instrument. It is regarded as the second most important instrument in China. Unlike the *qin*, which was considered an instrument of the nobility, the *pipa* has always been an instrument of the people. The word *pipa* is used to describe all instruments that are plucked by hand (in the style of a guitar). Today it is used in all types of Chinese music, especially folk ballads and opera. It is particularly exciting when played in a virtuosic way or when it is used to portray a dramatic battle.

- *Erhu* (*erwu*): a two-stringed fiddle played with a bow placed between the strings. It dates back 1000 years.

- *Yang chin* (*yang qin*): a zither plucked by two bamboo sticks.

- *Chin chin*: a three-stringed lute.

Wind instruments

- *Di* (*ti*): a small bamboo flute originally end-blown but now played horizontally. It has six finger-holes and another covered with rice paper which creates a particular buzzing sound. A type of mirliton.

- *Xiao* (*hsiao*): an endblown vertical flute.

- *Sona*: a double reed instrument, similar to an oboe, originally from Turkey.

• *Sheng*: a mouth organ made up of a gourd from which numerous small bamboo pipes protrude. The sound is made by blowing into the bowl. The Japanese *sho* and Korean *shaenghwang* are its descendants.

Drums

• *Kunqu* (*kun chu* or *chung ku*): small hourglass drums.

♪Listening

'The River Flowing' is played on *erhu* and *yang chin*. Notice playing techniques — the use of slides, trills, etc. This is a pentatonic piece.

Vocal music

Vocal music is an important and highly prized art throughout China. Some of the earliest Chinese music consisted of Buddhist chants, accompanied by bells, gongs and cymbals, which are about nine hundred years old. China has a long tradition of story-telling set to music — folk ballads, dramas, folk operas and formal operas. All are still very popular today. Chanting stories to the rhythmic accompaniment of a simple instrument such as the *pipa* is considered an art form and is called *shuo ch'ang*.

A bamboo flute

A type of *sheng*

A Beijing opera singer. Notice the elaborate costume and make-up

Hsi ch'u is a form of musical drama of which Beijing opera is the best example. Chinese opera has about three hundred regional variants but Beijing opera is the most popular. It combines the arts of acting, mime, acrobatics and costume, as well as singing and dancing.

The roles are stylised:

Sheng: the male role
Dan: the female role
Jing: character with the painted face
Chou: the clown

The arias and the singing styles are also stylised: the male usually sings in a raspy voice and the female sings in a high, nasal falsetto. They are accompanied on stage by a small orchestra consisting of *pipa*, fiddles, wind instruments (flutes and *sona*), drums, cymbals and clappers. The stories are based on history and folk tales, domestic situations and wars.

Chinese music has had a long history. It has influenced much of the philosophy behind music in Asia, as well as instrumentation and performing styles. It has been, in turn, influenced by music from other countries which it has now absorbed.

Here is a Chinese folk tune.

Wagon Driver's Tune

Chinese Folk Tune

Notice that it is pentatonic using the scale  and uses the

rhythm a number of times.

Some suggested accompaniments are included below

Woodblocks   Xylophone   Plucked Strings

Questions

1. Chinese music is classified into four periods. What are they?
2. What is the scale that most traditional music is based on?
3. Chinese music is defined as being heterophonic. What does this mean?
4. The philosopher Confucius divided music into two types — *ya* and *su*. What sort of music was each type?
5. Confucius also classified instruments according to the eight elements of the universe. This classification is found throughout many Asian countries. What are the eight categories?
6. What is meant by 'Sinocisation'?
7. How many variants of Chinese opera exist?
8. What are the four main roles in Beijing opera?
9. What instruments are used to accompany Beijing opera?
10. Describe these instruments briefly.

Japan

The origins of Japanese music date back well over one thousand years to the Shinto chants (Shintoism is the ancient Japanese religion in which nature is worshipped). Buddhism, the religion of China, came to Japan around the 4th century (300 AD) with its own chants. The two religions have coexisted ever since and their music has interacted.

About this same time, Japanese music (songs, instruments and style) was influenced not only by China but by other countries including Korea and India. Both China and Korea sent musicians and instruments to Japan, and by the 6th century, Japanese court musicians were sent to China and Korea to study the art of music.

For hundreds of years after that, Japan became very nationalistic, developing its own particular style of music. It was not until the mid 1800s, when Japan decided to Westernise, that any other major influences changed Japanese music. Today, Japan maintains its traditional cultural and musical roots together with Western music. Traditional native Japanese sacred music (*kangura*) is still played at religious festivals, and the ritualised court music, some of which dates back as far as 500 AD, is also still heard, unchanged over the centuries.

Gagaku (literally meaning 'elegant music') is the term used to describe all ancient, ritual Japanese music — singing, dancing as well as instrumental. When it is purely instrumental it is called *kangen* and when it involves singing or dancing it is called *bugaku*. *Gagaku* came into Japan from the imperial courts of China and Korea between 500 and 700 AD. The term *kugaku* described the music of the ordinary people — folk songs, thought of as vulgar by the nobility.

There are three main kinds of *gagaku*. Firstly, those ancient dances and songs that are Japanese in origin; secondly, music that was imported from Japan's Asian neighbours; and thirdly, music which was composed in imitation of other countries' styles. It gradually lost its popularity with the nobility of Japan but continued to be performed in the court of the emperor and at a few shrines and temples until the present day.

Gagaku is a slow, stately and flowing style of music and dance. Melodies are not written down but learnt by rote and the profession of *gagaku* musician is handed down from father to son. A *gagaku* ensemble is made up of strings, wind instruments and percussion. The music is heterophonic, which means that all the instruments play the same basic melody, though each may vary the tune slightly either rhythmically or melodically. The overall effect is one of a gracefully played and performed work achieving the maximum effect from the minimum material.

Japanese music employs timbres, pitch systems and rhythms which are different to those found in European music. The music is basically pentatonic — built on a five note scale. These scales or modes vary according to the type of music to be played or the mood that is to be created. The two most common modes are the 'In-mode' (or *insempo*) which has a minor sound and the 'Yo-mode' (*yosempo*).

Insempo   Yosempo

◁ The Japanese bamboo flute, the *shakuhachi*

Insempo is generally used for music which contains elaborate melodies while simple melodies are written in *yosempo*.

Melodic lines are varied in performance by ornamentation — turns, shakes and glissandi. Most Japanese music is in 2/4 meter, although rhythms in general are free or elastic and can be varied by the performer. The emotions or feelings created are of utmost importance rather than maintaining a regular pulse.

To Western ears, Japanese music may seem formless, but songs are often in an A–B (binary) form, while instrumental music occurs as an extended set of sections or variations on a theme (*dan*). Works for the *koto* (a traditional stringed zither) are usually written as *dan*.

Japanese music is divided into three parts, which attempt to reflect the seasonal changes that occur in nature:

jo: a quiet passage of increasing tension, followed by —
ha: an outburst of energy, which leads into —
kyu: a concentration of this energy into a single point of expression.

Music in Japan has always been closely related to drama. Songs and recitatives based on folk tales that are hundreds of years old are still performed. From these beginnings developed Japanese theatre music: *noh*, *kabuki* and *bunraku*.

A *bunraku* performance

Noh (or *no*) is a highly formalised style of drama which dates back to the 14th century. It is written in an ancient form of Japanese and the themes are about morality, with each play teaching right from wrong. Performances take place on a stage with a highly polished floor and no scenery. The actors wear elaborate masks and their movements are dramatic and stylised. Their dialogue (recitative) and songs are accompanied by an onstage ensemble of drums, which maintain a regular beat throughout the action, strings (*shamisens*), flute and a chorus singing in unison.

Kabuki is another type of music theatre. It developed from *noh* drama and a type of puppet theatre called *bunraku*, and is still popular today. The actors (men play all the roles) wear exotic costumes and wigs, and dramatic facial make-up and use lots of melodramatic and theatrical props. The story-lines are often historical (based on old Japanese tales) and, like *noh*, often deal with the conflict between duty and desire, but *kabuki* can also be humorous. The plot is narrated by singers accompanied by the string *shamisen*, gongs and bells.

Bunraku is Japanese puppet theatre that began in the 17th century. The puppets used today are very old (some two hundred years old), almost life-size, and are manipulated by puppeteers in view of the audience. The story is accompanied by a singer and *shamisen* player at the side of the stage. The art of *bunraku* is to effortlessly merge the story-telling with the actions of the puppets and the accompanying music.

♪ Listening

'Echigojishi' originally accompanied *kabuki* dances, but is now played as a concert work. Instruments include voices, *shamisen*, flute and drums. This piece is in a number of short sections, each differing in tempo, instrumentation and character. Notice the range and singing style of the men.

Instruments

Many of the instruments found in Japanese music originated in China or Korea and, as in those countries, were originally categorised according to the Confucian system of eight elements — stone, wood, bamboo, gourd, silk, leather, earth or clay and metal.

The main instruments are:

String instruments

- *Koto*: Though originally descended from the Chinese *qin* or *ch'in* around 600 AD, this zither is regarded as Japan's national instrument. It has thirteen strings of waxed silk (though today they are usually nylon) stretched lengthwise over a hollow wooden soundboard. The strings are tuned to the pentatonic scale over a range of two and a half octaves, using movable bridges. The performer sits in front of the *koto* and strokes and plucks the strings with ivory plectra that are worn over the thumb and index fingers of the right hand. The left hand varies the pitch of each string by pressing down on, or pulling up, the strings. The music for *koto* consists of a series of variations, or *dan*, and the melody itself often consists of wide leaps together with various performance ornamentation — glissandi, trills and arpeggios.

A *koto* player. Notice the bridges, the player's hand positions and the plectra on his right hand

- *Shamisen*: A three-stringed lute with a long thin neck which is held like a guitar. The left-hand fingers change the pitch of the note by pressing the string down onto the fingerboard. The right hand holds a plectrum with which the strings are plucked. It is used to accompany singing and drama.
- *Biwa*: A pear-shaped lute which, like the *shamisen*, came from China. It has four strings, is held like a guitar and played with a plectrum. It plays an important role in *gagaku* ensembles.

♪Listening

'Chidori' is a traditional work for *kotos*, *shamisen* and flute. The tempo is slow. The overall impression is that of an elegant and graceful combination of sounds. Notice the harmonies achieved. 'Chidori' is a good example of heterophony, with several instruments all playing variations on the main tune.

Wind instruments

They are made of bamboo and include:

- *Hichiriki*: a double reed oboe-like instrument. It is endblown and has nine finger-holes.
- *Ryuteki*: a horizontally held (transverse) flute with seven finger-holes.
- *Shakuhachi*: a stout, endblown flute about one metre long. It has four finger-holes at the front, a thumb-hole at the back and a sharp mouthpiece. It is tuned to the penta-tonic scale. It came to Japan from China during the 8th century and, like the *koto*, became popular around the 17th century when wandering and lawless samurai roamed the

country disguised as monks. They used the *shakuhachi* not only as an instrument but also as a handy weapon. It is capable of producing interesting nuances of sound when in the hands of an expert and is used for both solo and ensemble performances.

- *Sho*: a mouth-organ consisting of a gourd bowl with seventeen pipes standing in it. Similar to the Chinese *sheng* and Korean *shaenghwang*.

Drums and percussion

- *Taiko*: a small floor drum that is played with sticks. It is most often used for festival music and to accompany dances.
- *Daiko*: large barrel drums suspended from a stand or mounting. Used in *gagaku* and *kabuki*.
- *Tsuzumi*: hourglass drums. The *ko tsuzumi* is held on the shoulder and the *o tsuzumi* is a side-drum. They are both extremely important in the accompaniment of *noh* drama.
- Gongs, bells, clappers and cymbals are other important percussion instruments used for ceremonial, ritual and ensemble works.

A *biwa* player

Japanese school students learning to play the bamboo flute

Ryōtsu Jinku

Japanese Folk Song

Ai ga fukanu ka, ni ga nōte konu ka?
Tadasha Niigata no, yon-ya, kawadome ka?

Chidori, nake, nake. Washa tōdai de
Hoshi o nagamete, yon-ya, nezu no ban.

Omōte kita ka yo? Omowade koryoka,
Misawa yosawa no, yon-ya, sawa koete?

Notice the ornamentation of the melody line and the narrow vocal range (a fifth). The melody could be described as undulating or wave-like in shape.

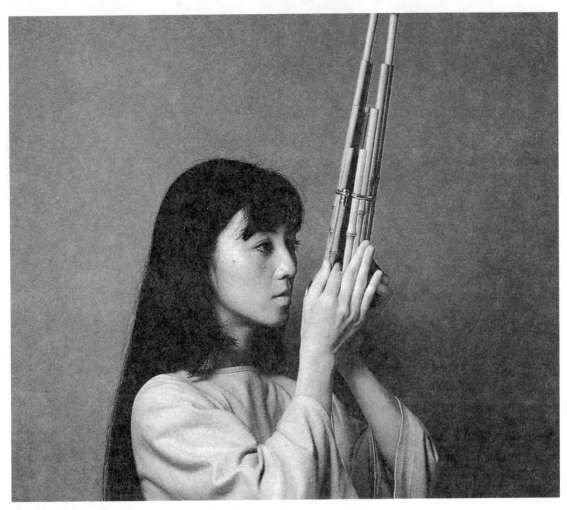

The *sho*. Compare this instrument to the Chinese *sheng*

Questions

1. Which two countries had the most influence on the development of Japanese music?
2. What is *gagaku*?
3. What are the two styles of *gagaku*?
4. What is *kugaku*?
5. Japanese music is heterophonic. What does this mean?
6. What is the basic scale and its two forms that are used in Japanese music?
7. When a Japanese musician plays music, he attempts to produce three distinctive sounds: *jo*, *ha*, *kyu*. Describe each one briefly.
8. What is *noh*, *kabuki* and *bunraku*?
9. Classify these instruments as to whether they are aerophones, membranophones, idiophones or chordophones:
   taiko, *ryuteki*, *sho*, *koto*, *hichiriki*, *biwa*.

Korea

Situated geographically between China and the islands of Japan, Korea is one of the oldest civilisations in the East. Culturally, all three have influenced each other in many ways, yet the music of each has remained distinctive and individual.

Korean music (*ak*) is divided into two broad categories: *a-ak* (also known as *chong-ak*, *chong* meaning right) was initially music considered right or correct for the ruling class; and *sog-ak*, music of the ordinary people.

Within each of these two divisions are two subcategories:

1. *A-ak* was originally introduced from China around the 5th century. It was music based on that of the Chinese imperial court and Confucian philosophy, namely that music's role was to express the harmony between man and the spiritual world. It used the pentatonic (and later, around the 8th century, the heptatonic) tonal systems. *A-ak* included the songs, dances and instrumental music used in the courts of the nobility — it was used to accompany courtly rituals, banqueting, and military occasions. Korea also developed its own classical native or indigenous music which was considered as belonging to this category and it is known as *hyang-ak*.

2. *Sog-ak* belonged to the people rather than the ruling class and is also of two types: ritual music such as religious songs, dances and instrumental music of the Buddhist temples and the ancient magician-priests (shamans); and folk music. Korea has long been an agricultural nation and much of this folk music, in the form of songs as well as dances, is concerned with farming (*non-ak*). Secular vocal music is also of several styles, and can be performed either accompanied or unaccompanied. *Pansori*, a long one-man opera or chanted narrative, is regarded as a national treasure because of its historical importance.

Korean music is generally based on the pentatonic (five note) scale but because the playing and singing style uses a vibrato around the note, the sound does not seem 'precise'. As with the music of China and Japan, instruments playing together produce heterophony, that is, simultaneous versions of the same melody.

Vocal music varies in its character. Ritual music is often formalised, and sung in a slow stylised way, with the syllables of each word extended, or drawn out. In contrast, other vocal music found in Korea, especially that of folk music, can be fast and syncopated, with a sound more Indian than oriental.

The rhythms of court music are elastic, and there is no regular beat. As with Chinese and Japanese music, it is the feeling of the music that is most important rather than its rhythmic preciseness. The rhythms of folk dances, on the other hand, are fast, bright and very rhythmic, the beat maintained by gongs and drums.

♪ Listening

'Kyung Bok Kung Thoryung' is an example of Korean folk music — a song accompanied by a combination of percussion and wind instruments. The song uses a pentatonic scale and is very bright and rhythmic. The time signature is 3/4 and there is a regular four bar cycle, emphasised by the heavy down-beat on the first note of every fourth bar. What do you notice about the style of singing?

◁ Traditional court musicians. Notice the similarity between the bowed zither and the Japanese *koto*

A harvest celebration dance with a variety of drums as accompaniment

Dance, like singing or playing an instrument, is considered one of the main forms of interpreting and performing music. There are a huge variety of dances, both *a-ak* and *sog-ak*. Many ritual dances are very old, some dating back to the 2nd century, and are usually based on some Confucian or religious philosophy. Court dances are generally very graceful and expressive of inner feelings, with each movement implying some meaning. The costumes are colourful and elegant. Many of these dances take place in a circle and the tempos are generally slow. Folk dances have varying tempos, but are frequently fast and the movements are joyful and often improvised.

Instruments

Korea has a rich variety of musical instruments, traditionally made of the eight elements as prescribed by Confucian doctrine. They include:

- metal   *pyonjong*: a set of sixteen bronze bells
          panghyang: bell chimes
          ching: gong
          nabal: brass trumpet
- stone   *pyongyong*: a set of sixteen stone chimes suspended in a frame
          tukyong: single stone chime

- silk   *kayagum*: twelve-stringed zither
            komungo: six-stringed zither
            haegum: two-stringed fiddle
- bamboo   *piri*: an oboe-like instrument with a double reed
            taegum: large transverse or horizontal flute
- gourd   *shaenghwang*: mouth organ similar to Chinese *sheng* and Japanese *sho*
- clay   *hoon*: globular flute
            boo: clay jar struck with a mallet
- skin   drums such as the
            changgu: hourglass drum
            chwago: barrel drum
- wood   *eo*: wooden rasp in the shape of a tiger
            pak: a set of wooden clappers

Musicians accompany a traditional ceremony at a royal ancestral shrine Notice the *pyongyong* on the right

A musician plays the *kayagum*

The following instruments are the most representative of Korean music:

- *Taegum*: A large transverse or horizontal flute. It has a blowing hole: a hole covered by a thin membrane (a mirliton) which makes the tone very expressive, six finger-holes and five other holes. This instrument is found in most Korean musical ensembles.

- *Komungo*: A six-stringed zither which is plucked with a bamboo rod in the right hand, while the left presses on the strings to create changes of tones.

- *Kayagum*: This is related to the Chinese *cheng* and the Japanese *koto* and is a twelve-stringed zither. The right-hand fingers pluck the strings while the left fingers alter the string tensions. Played in stately court music and also the fast, energetic folk music.

- *Piri*: A double reed 'oboe', favoured as a leading instrument in court music and folk ensembles.

'Arirang' is one of the most popular Korean folk songs. It is built on the pentatonic scale and is characterised by the lilting dotted crotchet-quaver rhythm.

Arirang

Korean Folk Song

A - ri-rang, A - ri-rang, A - ra - ri - yo____

A - ri-rang Ko - ge - ro,____ Nŏ - mŏ-gan - da.

Na - rŭl pŏ - ri - go, Ka - shinŭn nim - ŭn,____

Shim - ni - do mot - ga - sŏ,____ Pal - byŏng-nan - da.

Questions

1. Korean music (*ak*) is divided into two main categories. Give the correct Korean names and their English equivalents.
2. Each of the two categories can be subdivided still further. Complete the table:

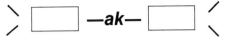

3. What country had the greatest influence on Korean music?
4. Which country did Korea influence the most?
5. Name the two most important Korean chordophones. What are the main differences between them?
6. What is the most obvious difference between traditional Korean court dances and folk dances of the people?
7. What is the most obvious difference between ritual vocal music and that of Korean folk songs?
8. What is *hyang-ak*?
9. *Pansori* can be described as . . .?
10. Which one of the eight Confucian categories does each of these instruments fit into? What is their Sachs–Hornbostel equivalent?
    piri, ching, boo, eo, pyongyong, changgu, komungo

Vietnam

Vietnam is one of the nations of Indo-China and has always been influenced by Chinese culture. It is not surprising, therefore, that the instruments and scales used in Vietnamese music will be similar to those used in Chinese music. Overall, Vietnamese society is a blend of a number of religions (including Buddhism, Taoism, Confucianism and Animism), and is made up of people from distinct racial areas: Tonkinese, from the north, and Annamites, from the south. These factors, and the rule of the French from 1884 until the mid 20th century, have created a 'melting pot' effect which is reflected in different types and roles of music in Vietnam.

Another reason for the various musical styles is the fact that the melodic line of songs must follow the rise and fall of speech. Vietnamese is a tonal language, which means that the same word can mean different things depending on the pitch, or tone, given to it. As there are different dialects, this means that the music for each dialect group must be different as it has to mirror the tones of speech.

Like so much Asian music, Vietnamese music is pentatonic. But the applications of the pentatonic idea include different scales and ways of using them. Two basic scales exist, *bać* and *nam*.

Bać can be notated as

and is considered to represent a happy sound. This scale, under different names, is also used in China, Mongolia, Korea and Japan.

Nam can be notated as

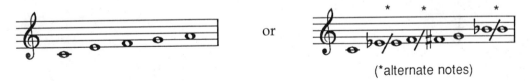

(*alternate notes)

and is seen as expressing sadness.

In *bać* scale, any note can be the final note, and transpositions are allowed. For example,

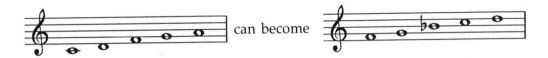

can become

Transposition, options on final notes, and chromatically varied tones in the *nam* scale lead to a range of musical possibilities that can break the usual restrictions of a rigidly applied pentatonic system. The transpositions of scales also have mood implications, for example this version of *nam* is one of the most unhappy:

◁ The *dàn ty ba*.

An important element of Vietnamese music is the use of spontaneous elaboration and improvisation as the music is performed. This is called *hoa-la* (flowering) and results in distinctive heterophonic interpretations of melodies. Improvisation is also used to provide introductory passages to pieces during which the notes of the scale to be used, and thus the mood of the piece, are introduced.

(L to R): Musicians perform on the *dàn ty ba*, *dàn tranh* and flute.

Types of music

Dàn Tranh

This is the repertoire of the *dàn tranh*, a small sixteen-stringed zither introduced from China in the 10th century. The style of performance is similar to Japanese *koto* playing: the right hand uses specific techniques including sliding, vibrato, jumping, and plucking, while the left hand performs delicate ornamental effects peculiar to Vietnamese music.

The *dàn tranh* has always been a popular instrument for young girls to play, and can be played solo or in groups. The repertoire consists of ancient folk material and modern compositions (for example, by modern Vietnamese composer Tran Quang Hai). Often the playing of a piece is preceded by an improvised section to set the mood and introduce the particular form of scale being used.

Hat a Dao

This North Vietnamese sung poetry dates from before the 15th century and was originally ceremonial, accompanying dancing and acrobatics. It grew in importance, becoming a high art form for the performance of lyric poetry, not only of Vietnamese origin but also of poetry translated from Chinese literature. Because it is very intellectual, it is fading from Vietnamese musical culture.

Like *dàn tranh* music, improvising within the conventions of the scales is an important part of its style.

Cai Luong

In 1917 a group of southern Vietnamese created this new art form when they performed a short 'opera' using existing tunes to act out a simple story. The idea quickly caught on and grew into an accepted and popular style of entertainment, combining singing, music, costumes, and acting. The stories are taken from all types of sources: Vietnamese culture, Chinese literature, and 19th century European novels, among others.

One particular song, 'Vong Cổ', is so popular that it is used in nearly every *cai luong* and is the basis for improvisation and variation. There are also conventional songs to accompany certain dramatic events.

Instruments

Vietnamese music is not dominated by tuned percussion ensembles as are found in Indonesia and other areas of South-East Asia. The instruments, because of the ancient connections with Chinese culture, are similar to those used in Chinese music. They include:

String instruments
- *dàn tranh*: a sixteen-stringed zither
- *yang k'in*: a dulcimer of thirty-six strings
- *dàn ty ba* and *dàn nguyet*: lutes
- *dàn nhi*: a two-stringed fiddle
- guitars on which the frets have been altered to accommodate Vietnamese scales

Wind instruments
- *sona*: oboe
- *kouan*: clarinet
- *ken*: shawm

Percussion
- gongs
- drums

Notice the use of the word '*dàn*', Vietnamese for 'instrument', in some of these names.

The *dàn nhi*

♪ Listening

Listen to the medley of three Vietnamese songs on the tape. This is performed by an ensemble of Vietnamese stringed and percussion instruments. Notice the glissando effect typical of the *dan tranh* and the heterophonic effect which uses independent elaboration in each instrumental part. This music is in the *bać* scale.

Folk songs

As in many societies, folk songs and dances are an important cultural component in Vietnam, and they are functional, being performed at weddings, funerals, etc. Here are two examples of folk songs. Notice that they are pentatonic and are each made up of short melodic ideas that are repeated.

Hát Hội Trăng Răm

Vietnamese Folk Song
Transcribed by P. D. H.

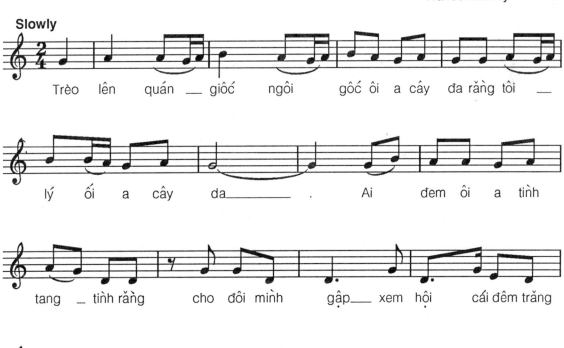

Cò Lả

North Vietnamese Traditional Song
Transcribed by P. D. H.

Questions

1. a. What other Asian country has strongly influenced Vietnamese music?
   b. How is this influence shown?
2. What factors contribute to the 'melting pot' effect in Vietnamese culture?
3. Why are Vietnamese regional songs so different?
4. a. What scale is used in Vietnamese music?
   b. Name two different versions of this scale, and say how their moods differ.
5. What is *dàn tranh* music?
6. Since what time has *hat a dao* been performed?
7. a. When did *cai luong* begin?
   b. What song is used in most *cai luong* performances?
8. List the instruments of Vietnamese music under the following headings: string, wind, percussion.

9. a. What is the Vietnamese word for 'instrument'?
    b. List two instruments that include this word in their names.
10. What is meant by 'functional folk music'?
11. What type of scale do both examples of folk song use?
12. What is *hoa-la*? What effect does it have on performance?

A Vietnamese monochord

Indonesia

Music is a very important part of Indonesian life, not only in its use in villages for social occasions and entertainment, but also for its links to religion and the way that it is seen as a connection between everyday life and the cosmos. Indonesia has a wide range of musical styles. We will look at four of them: *gamelan* music, *kroncong*, *dangdut*, and folk song.

Gamelan music

The word *gamelan* is used to name an ensemble of instruments, the music it plays, and sometimes the idea of 'music' itself. As an ensemble, a *gamelan* is a unique Indonesian group made up of mostly tuned percussion instruments of metal. A *gamelan* can have from about six to fifty players, though large ones are rare. The most usual size is about twelve to twenty players.

What makes the *gamelan* such a unique concept is not only its make-up of tuned percussion, but also its own system of music composition. This is known as colotomic structure. This structure can best be explained by saying that each instrument in a *gamelan* has its own specific role which fits into the overall sound like pieces fit into a jigsaw. These roles are related to melody and rhythm and are governed by the pitch of the instruments.

Gamelan music is arranged in pitch layers and is based around a central theme which is played over and over. The high-pitched instruments play their version of the theme in rapid notes, the middle-range instruments play it at a medium speed, and the low-range instruments play a slow version of it. Because the individual instruments in a *gamelan* exist in different sizes — called *panerus* (smallest), *barung* (middle), and *slentem* (largest — we can show this colotomy in the following way:

Large gongs punctuate this structure at the ends of the musical phrases and a drum, or drums, played by the leader of the *gamelan*, sets the speeds.

Here is a piece of Balinese *gamelan* music, 'Baris Bapan', traditionally played to accompany a men's dance, the *baris*. Notice that it only uses four notes and shows colotomic structure by its layers of pitch related to speed, and the melodic outline. (It can be played on tuned percussion, xylophones and glockenspiels.)

◁ The *rebab*

Baris Bapan

Balinese Gamelan
Transcribed by P.D.H.

Gamelans throughout Indonesia are not standard in size, type of instruments used, tuning, or in the sounds they produce. There are three main types:

1. The Javanese *gamelan* can be traced back to the 7th century and originally existed in two forms: soft for indoors and loud for outdoors. In Java no royal court was complete without at least one *gamelan*. The sound of the Javanese *gamelan* is sedate and ordered, and sometimes includes bamboo instruments alongside metal ones.

2. Sundanese (West Javanese) *gamelans* are smaller than Javanese and use non-percussion instruments — the *suling* (bamboo flute) and *rebab* (two-stringed fiddle) — with the usual percussion ones.

3. Balinese *gamelans* are perhaps the best known type of *gamelan*. Their sound is exciting and more vibrant than either the Javanese or Sundanese because they use predominantly metal instruments. As well, their instruments are tuned slightly out-of-tune with each other and this gives their music a ringing effect. Also, they are played with much more vigour and their music is more dramatic, using sudden contrasts of speed and volume.

Listening

Listen to 'Selir', an example of Balinese *gamelan* on the tape. This music is a traditional ceremonial piece played during religious festivals and shows the idea of colotomy. Notice the punctuation of the gongs and the different speeds of the instruments. Compare this piece to the example of Javanese *gamelan* on the tape. The Javanese piece is untitled, its *gamelan* is smaller and uses a different set of instruments, including *rebab*, *suling*, and singing.)

A small Balinese *gamelan* comprising: 1. a hanging gong; 2. *trompongs*; 3. *genders*; 4. *kendangs* (drums)

Gamelan instruments

It is difficult to consistently name the instruments used in *gamelan* because they vary depending on whether they are Javanese (which includes Sundanese) or Balinese. Remember that each instrument can exist in three sizes: *panerus, barung, slentem*. In this list the Balinese name is given first, with the Javanese name included in brackets. The instruments are of two types:

Gongs
- *trompong* (*bonang/kenong*): a set of small gongs resting in a wooden frame
- *kendang*: one small gong resting on a box
- large single gongs hanging in a frame.

In Bali the large gongs are *lanang* (male) and *wadon* (female), in Java they are called *ageng, suwukan*, and *kempul*.

Metal bars
- *jegogan* (*gender*)
- *saron* (*saron*)

Other instruments

- *cheng cheng*: a set of small cymbals mounted on a base and played continually to provide a beat
- *suling*
- *rebab*
- *celempung*: small zither
- *anklung*: tuned bamboo rattle
- *gambang*: a bamboo xylophone

Indonesian music uses two tuning systems (called *laras*):

slendro, which is pentatonic, e.g.

pelog, a seven note scale, e.g.

Within each of these there are sub-scales, or modes, called *patets* which imply certain melodic formulae and can correspond to moods and times of the day or night. In Java there is a special type of *gamelan* called the royal *gamelan* which has two sets of instruments, one in each *lara* set at right angles so the *gamelan* can change from *slendro* to *pelog*.

A *saron*, with a *gender* behind. Notice that the *saron* has the five notes of the pentatonic scale

A musician plays the *suling*

Other types of music

Kroncong

This is a type of Javanese folk music, considered high quality, which developed from the songs that Portuguese sailors brought to Indonesia from the 16th century on. The links to Portuguese music are evident in the accompaniment of *kroncong* songs which is played on plucked string instruments, types of guitars, etc. The Indonesian word '*kroncong*' means small string instrument.

Dangdut

Dangdut is a type of street music which derives its name onomatopoetically from its drum rhythms, which come from Indian music. *Dangdut* must include drumming, though any other instrument can be used as well. It is considered a low type of music and is often played by beggars in the large cities.

Buka Pintu

Folk songs

Folk songs developed from European models are sung in Indonesia. Unlike the indigenous music, they are not based on authentic Indonesian scales, for example *pelog* and *slendro*, but on European chordal harmony. They are usually simple, with repetitive verse structure, often use nonsense syllables, and can be satirical or humorous. The song 'Buka Pintu' is an example of this style.

Music has very strong functional uses in Indonesia. It is essential in religious ceremonies, and *gamelans* accompany entertainments such as dances, the *wayang kulit* (shadow puppet plays), *wayang golek* (puppet plays), and *arja* ('operas').

Questions

1. What is meant by the word '*gamelan*'?
2. a. What is colotomic structure?
   b. How does the pitch of an instrument decide its role in the colotomic structure?
3. What are the three sizes of an instrument called and what sizes are they?
4. What is the difference between Javanese, Sundanese, and Balinese *gamelans*?
5. a. What are the two scales used in Indonesian music and how many notes has each?
   b. What is a *patet* and what is its implication?
6. What is *kroncong* and which European country does its style reflect?
7. How did *dangdut* get its name and what instrument must it contain?
8. What style of music are folk songs based on?
9. What do *gamelans* accompany?
10. List all the instruments mentioned in this topic under the following headings: percussion, string, wind.

Balinese drummers.

India

The Indian word for music is *sangita*. Some of the oldest music in Asia has been discovered in India and Indian music has influenced the music of other countries in the region (including China, Korea and Japan). In turn, it has been influenced by music and culture from its Muslim-Arabic neighbours.

The voice has always been very important in Indian music. Religion, the supernatural, the spiritual, gods and philosophy, too, have a long association with music. Legend has it that the god Brahma first taught music in the form of songs to humans. It is not surprising, then, that the earliest music was vocal and religious in character. The hymns of the Rig Veda are 3000 years old, and were three note chants to the deities or gods. Songs of the Samaveda are also ancient and were built on five, six and seven note melodies.

These Vedic hymns told of the universe, how it was made and the laws of nature that functioned within the universe. The very sound of the words themselves reinforced the universal truths. For example, *agni* (pronounced ugni), the first word of the Rig Veda is built on three sounds which explain the universe:

a: first sound an infant makes. It implies the primeval energy which was the beginning of all things

g: a gutteral sound which cuts off or puts an end to the universe's first energy

ni: the energy of the universe as we know it.

With these hymns or chants, music in India began to be formalised or given a structure.

Indian music is melodic. That is, like its neighbours China and Japan, its music is based wholly on melodies which are then varied by decorative improvisation. This is different to Western music which is harmonic, or built upon changing chord patterns. As we have seen, some of the first Indian melodies or chants are very old, and by about the 3rd century BC, a scale was in use not unlike our C scale. But then, as now, this scale was varied by making use of quartertones between the notes, and emphasising unusual intervals.

Traditional Indian music does not use major and minor scales as used in the West, rather, *ragas* are the melodic building blocks. A *raga* (or *rag*) is a fixed tonal sequence — part scale, part melody — upon which the performer elaborates in a series of variations. The word *raga* comes from a Sanskrit word meaning 'to please'. There are more than three hundred *ragas*, each one expressing a particular mood or emotion of Hindu philosophy such as love, tranquillity, anger, adoration, merriment and mystery. Each *rag* is associated with or played at a particular time of day, and each *rag* has a name relating to its origin (the person who wrote it, where it came from or its mood). A professional musician must know at least one hundred of them, and Indian audiences know many of them as well.

Ragas have a variable number of notes and these may differ according to whether the *raga* is ascending or descending. Even if two *ragas* share the same notes, they will differ according to mood, which notes are accented as well as the microtonal shadings between notes. In Western music, the smallest intervals between any two notes is a semi (1/2) tone, Indian music makes use of much smaller intervals — *sruti* — and there may be more than twenty of these minute or microtonal intervals in an octave. They are difficult for Western listeners to detect, but accepted as natural by Indians. As well, the way of moving from one note to another and the playing of it can vary (e.g. shakes, trills, glides, turns, glissandi and grace notes).

◁A Hindustani musician performs on the two- stringed lute

The famous Indian *sitar* player, Ravi Shankar. Notice the *tambura* behind him.

Just as a *raga* is a note row from which the melody is made, the rhythmic basis of Indian music is the *tala* (or *tal*). A *tal* is a rhythmic pattern or fixed cycle of beats which is improvised upon. As with *ragas*, there are several hundred rhythmic patterns, each one made up of any number of beats, the most popular *tala* having 6, 10, 12, 14 or 16 beats which are then subdivided into smaller divisions of time. The most important note of the cycle is the first, *sam*, and is the most emphasised. Other notes may be accented loudly or softly.

Try playing these *tals* (x – loudly, o – softly):

Tintal
x	x	o	x
1 2 3 4	5 6 7 8	9 10 11 12	13 14 15 16

Rupak
x	x	o
1 2 3	4 5	6 7

Dipchandi
x	x	o	x
1 2 3	4 5 6 7	8 9 10	11 12 13 14

Dadra
x	o
1 2 3	4 5 6

The form of a *raga* in performance is quite long, but it is in three definite parts:

Alap: slow introduction which states the *raga* and gives the mood (on the melody instrument)
Jor: the rhythmic accompaniment begins
Gat: an extended improvisatory section for both instruments which builds up in excitement and intensity to a climax (on the *sam*).

Beneath the competing melodic and rhythmic instruments lies the third layer of sound which distinguishes Indian music: the drone. This can be provided by an additional string instrument or by the melody instrument itself.

♪ Listening

Listen to the three excerpts from the 'Raga Muru-Behag' (an evening *raga* which 'expresses the sorrow of unfulfilled love') on the tape. The two instruments playing are the *sitar*, providing melody and drone, and *tabla*. The rhythmic pattern is the *tintal* (sixteen beats, given in the pattern above).

1. *Alap* : the sitar begins slowly, enunciating the *rag* and exploring its melodic possibilities. Notice the underlying drone produced by the sympathetic strings of the *sitar*.
2. *Jor*: the *tabla* enters as the third layer of sound. The *tabla* and *baya* produce contrasting but complementary tone colours (timbre) and pitches (the *tabla* high, the *baya* low).
3. *Gat*: is marked by accelerating tempo and increasing excitement.

Indian music is based on a series of repetitions and variations of the *raga* (scale) and *tala* (rhythmic patterns). Each repetition is more varied and decorated than the previous one. The three elements of Indian music — melody, rhythm and drone — are given for you in the following exercise to explore and develop. Practise each section independently before putting all the parts together. *Ragas* are characterised by a gradual acceleration in tempo.

1. The *raga* ('Malakosh', a night *raga*, peaceful and thoughtful in mood): Play on the recorder, tuned percussion, string instrument or voice.

2. Drone: Play on guitar, keyboard or low-tuned percussion.

3. The *tala* is the sixteen beat 'tintal'.

Play it on percussion instruments, drums or bongos.

	X				X				O				X			
	1	2	3	4	5	6	7	8	9	10	11	12	13	14	15	16
Instrument 1	X				X								X			
Instrument 2		X		X		X		X		X		X		X		X
Instrument 3	X		XX	X	X		XX	X			XX	X		XX	X	
Instrument 4		XX	X			XX	X			XX	X			XX	X	

Music Arr. R. Carter

Instruments

India is a huge continent and over time two musical streams have developed: the northern or Hindustani, which has been influenced by Persian, or Moghul, invasions and occupation around the 13th century; and the southern or Carnatic. Perhaps the most obvious difference between the two styles lies with the instruments. Hindustani music contains many instruments of Arabic or Persian descent, such as the *sitar, sarod, rabab, sarangi* and *tabla*.

Indian musicians playing the horizontal flute and *tabla* and *baya* (a pair of small drums)

String instruments

- *Sitar*: The instrument most identified with Indian music. This is a kind of long-necked lute which came to India from Persia about seven hundred years ago. (The word 'tar' gives its Arabic origins away. Another instrument descended from the same Arabic instrument, the *qitara*, is the guitar). It has between twenty and thirty-five metal strings, but only seven of these are used to play the melody. The others vibrate sympathetically to create the characteristic drone bass. The sitar has two sound chambers or gourds, one at either end of the long neck, and nineteen movable frets along the neck which allow the instrument to be tuned to a particular *rag*. The *sitar* is held like a guitar while the performer sits on the floor. The strings are plucked with a metal plectrum over the index finger of the right hand, while the fingers of the left hand press down on or pull the strings.

- *Vina* (or *veena*): The Carnatic equivalent of the *sitar*. It is a melody instrument and looks somewhat like the *sitar*, having a long neck with two gourds, one at either end. It has seven strings, four of them for playing the melody, and three drone strings. The *vina* is held horizontally, the melody being played by the fingernails (or plectrum) of the right hand while the little finger plucks the drone on the open strings. The *vina* has a three octave range and its tone is softer than that of the sitar.

A singer accompanies herself on the drone instrument, the *tambura*

- *Tambura*: A similar shape to the *vina* but with only one sound chamber. The strings are not stopped with the fingers of the left hand but are plucked by the right hand to create a drone-type accompaniment.
- *Sarangi*: This is another bowed instrument, but much older. It has three thick strings and produces a low mellow tone. It is considered an instrument of the lower castes and is found in ensembles which may accompany singing or dancing.
- Violin: A more recent addition to India's many instruments.

Percussion instruments

These also differ between the south and the north. They are of two types: membranophones (drums) and idiophones. Drums are the most popular accompanying instruments. Their skin heads are tuned by braces and wedges, and a black dot made of flour and iron filings is applied to alter the sound, making it deeper and more resonant. The art of good drumming is to vary the tone quality using the fingers and palms of the hands rather than to merely play loudly. Percussion instruments include:

- *damru*: (snake charmer's drum) a small hourglass or waisted drum with two balls attached to lengths of twine. They make a long drum roll when the drum is shaken.

- *mridanga*: found in the south, it is the oldest of all Indian drums. It is barrel-shaped and made of baked clay. It sits on the player's lap so that both heads can be played with the fingers.
- *tabla*: a pair of complementary drums with single heads — the *tabla* and the *baya*. The *tabla* is a small wooden drum and is played with the fingertips of the right hand. The *baya* is a fatter, rounder drum made of metal, usually copper, and is played with the left hand.
- cymbals (*mandira*): of various sorts. Rattles, bells and jingles add colour to folk music, and dancers often attach the latter to their ankles and wrists.

Wind instruments

These are often played unaccompanied or in ensembles or groups. They include:

- *pungi* or *been*: snake charmer's instruments. These are made of a gourd with two pipes attached, through which the player blows. Finger-holes allow changes of notes. The sound produced is harsh and drone-like.
- *sringa*: an S-shaped, curved instrument originally made of cow horn, and used in temples.
- *sahanai*: an oboe-like instrument with a metal bell, wooden bore and a double reed.
- flutes of various kinds are used throughout India. They can be endblown (like the *bansari*) or transverse.

Clarinets and squeezeboxes, like the violin, have been adopted from the West and adapted to Indian music. The violin and clarinet can be heard in ensembles while the squeezebox is used in temples to accompany singers.

Two *sahanai* and a drum

Dance

Dance is an important musical art in India. Many of the traditional folk dances are hundreds of years old. They often tell, with movement and expressive eye and body gestures, myths and legends of gods and the supernatural. Dance, like singing and instrumental music, is based on traditional themes and movements but the interpretation of a dance is up to the performer. Improvisation on the movements and conveying of the emotions and expressions of the dances and their moods are very important. The dancers often accompany their movements with singing.

Many dances are identified with certain areas, others with particular festivals or religious themes. Story-telling in dance, based on the 'Ramayana' and 'Mahabarata' (stories of the god Krishna and the battle between good and evil) is the foundation of many dance-dramas such as the 'Kathakali'. Other famous traditional dances include 'Odissi' (sensuous and lyrical dances originally based on a text about the Lord Krishna), 'Manipuri', 'Kathak' and the 'Bharata' (the oldest dance in India, and devotional in spirit).

Here is a traditional Indian song for you to perform. Add rhythms on finger cymbals as an accompaniment.

Raghupati

Indian Folk Song

A classical dance performance. Notice the stylised hand gestures.

Questions

1. What are the Vedic hymns?
2. Explain what is meant by *raga*.
3. What is the rhythmic basis of Indian music?
4. What is the *sam*?
5. *Alap*, *jor* and *gat* form the overall shape of the *raga* in performance. What happens in each section?
6. What are the principal instruments used in:
   a. Carnatic music?
   b. Hindustani music?
7. Which country influenced the music of the north from the 13th century? What evidence is there for this?
8. Which Western instruments have been adapted for playing traditional Indian music?
9. Indian music is based on improvisation. Explain the term 'improvise'.
10. Categorise these instruments according to the Sachs–Hornbostel method of classification: *bansari*, *mridanga*, *mandira*, *pungi*, *sahanai*, *sarengi*.

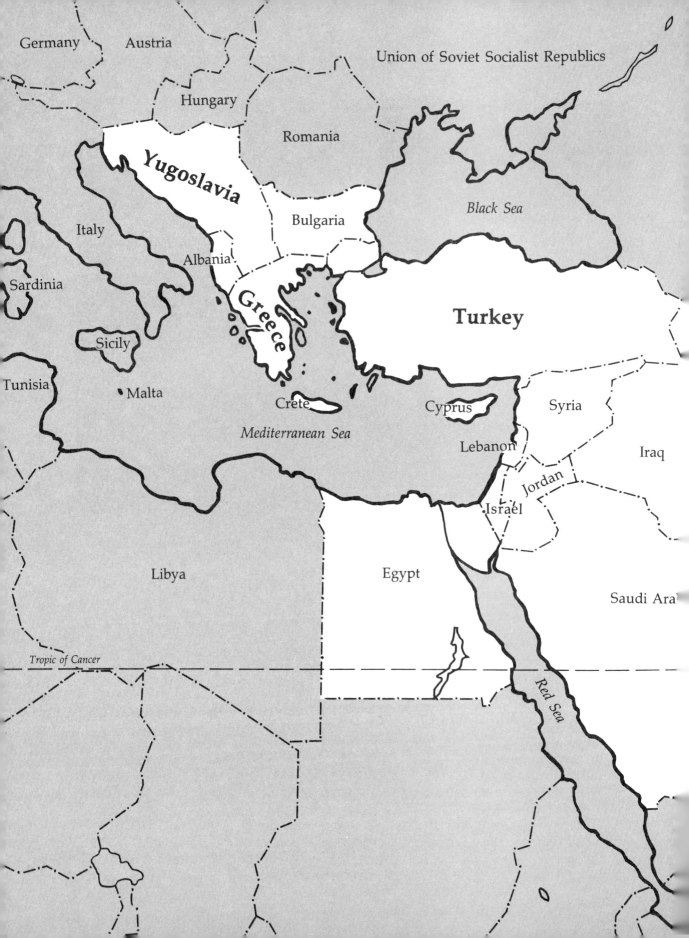

Caspian Sea

Iran

Kuwait

United
Arab Emirates

Indian Ocean

3

EASTERN
Mediterranean

Iran

Situated between Turkey and Pakistan and India, Iran (formerly Persia) links European and Asian music. This can be seen in the types and names of instruments in use in India and the rest of Asia, and in Eastern and Western Europe, that can be traced to instruments of Persian origin. The Persian *tar* and *setar* (plucked chordophones of the long-necked lute type) could be related to the Indian *sitar*, and the Spanish *guitarra*, while the Persian fiddle, the *rabab*, can be recognised in the Indonesian *rebab*, and the old European *rebec* (an ancestor of the modern violin).

The influence of music from the Middle East on European music in the Middle Ages is well known. For example, typically Eastern instruments — such as the double reed instruments which developed into the modern oboe and bassoon — were unknown in Europe until brought back by knights returning from the Crusades. Small drums, called *nakkers*, used in medieval European music were copied from Persian drums which today are still called *naqqara*.

Although officially frowned on by the religion of Islam, music is an important part of Iranian life. In religion it is used for the call to prayer (*azan*) which is sung out over the countryside, and as a means for children to learn the Koran by chanting passages from it. Non-religious music includes folk songs and dances, and traditional classical Iranian music called *radif*.

Folk songs are connected to everyday life by being about it, or by being functional (i.e. used for weddings, festivals, etc.). As well, there are epic songs which narrate historical events, performed by poet/musicians called *ashiq*, who accompany themselves on the *saz* (a long-necked lute). A similar tradition exists in Turkey (the *asik*) and in Yugoslavia (the *guslar*).

The love song, 'Kouh Beh Kouh', is a popular folk song. Notice the limited vocal range, the use of repetition, and the ornamental descending triplet figure (bars 2, 4, 5, 8) which gives the song its Eastern flavour.

Kouh Beh Kouh

◁ This 16th century Iranian painting shows musicians entertaining a ruler. Instruments pictured include the *ud*, *kemence*, *defs*, *sorna*, drums, and hand percussion

gousch - va - ré   dar ___ gousch   Hoi! _ hoi! _ hoi!

Ha-djar gra - shang   é   mast-o ma - lang - é___

2. Kouh beh kouh migardidam,   Djân! djân! djân!
    Az peiyé âhou,   Hadjar gaschang é,
    Yâré khodra man didam   Masto malang é!
    Pahlou beh pahlou,

Performance of these songs is mostly solo and often unaccompanied, though with instrumental interludes to separate the verses. This style can be heard in the listening example on the tape.

♪ Listening

In this love song the verses alternate with instrumental sections played on the *kemenche*, a three-stringed spike fiddle. Notice that the singer's part stays the same but the *kemenche* plays different music each time, though its relationship to the singer's melody can be heard. This demonstrates the concept of improvisation around a melody.

Classical Iranian music is called *radif*, and is based on a complex theory system. The two major elements are melody and rhythm:

1. The melody part of *radif* is associated with the *maqam*, best translated as 'mode' or 'scale', though *maqam* implies not only the notes that can be used but also melodic formulas and shapes which can be utilised in the performance of a piece. In this way we can see a link to the Indian theory of the *raga*. The term '*maqam*' is actually Arabic, and often the Persian word *avaz* is used as well. The individual scales are called *dastgah*. There are a number of *maqamati* with implications of time and mood.

2. Rhythm in *radif* is governed by the concept of *darb*, pre-determined rhythm patterns which are learnt by drummers through mnemonic syllable devices.

♪ Listening

Listen to the excerpt from a piece of *radif* on the tape. The instruments are a *santur* (dulcimer-type instrument) and *zarb* (goblet drum). The *dastgah* (scale) of this excerpt is *dastgah-e segah*, that is:

Notice the use of the sign ꞵ (*koron*, approximately half a flat) which demonstrates the problem of trying to notate music from another system onto the Western five line stave.

Radif relies on the skill of its performers to demonstrate their ability to improvise around the *dastgah* and to ornament the music as they play. The first tape example showed the same practice.

A musician plays the *santur*.

Instruments

The instruments of Iranian music include:

Drums

- *darabuk*: also called *zarb*, single headed goblet shape
- *dohol*: large bass drum
- *def*: frame drum with one skin and often with jingles attached, similar to a large tambourine
- *naqqara*: the small paired kettledrums

Bowed stringed instruments

- *kemenche*: three-stringed spike fiddle
- *geichek*: with one to three melody strings and several sympathetic strings
- *rabab* (fiddle): the word is applied to a range of bowed folk instruments with varying numbers of strings

Plucked string instruments

- lute types: these include the *tambur* (six strings), the *tar* (six strings), the *ud* (four to ten strings), and *saz* (three strings). Except for the *ud*, these have quite long necks.

Struck stringed instruments

- These include the *santur* (a trapezoid zither instrument with seventy-two strings, four to a note, struck by small sticks), and the *qanun* (also with seventy-two strings but plucked by plectra in the player's hands).

The *geichek*

The Iranian *setar* or *saz*. Compare this instrument to the Turkish *baglama* and the Greek *bouzouki*

Blown instruments

- *sorna*: oboe type
- *ney*: endblown flute
- *karna*: trumpet type
- *ney-arbun*: bagpipe

The pairing of *sorna* and *dohol* is standardised for certain dances and is an important part of village festivities, as the same combination is in Turkey (*davul–zurna*) and Yugoslavia (*zurle–goč*).

Questions

1. What Persian instruments can be linked to those in India, Indonesia and Europe? To what instruments do they relate?
2. What are *naqqara*? What medieval European instrument is copied from them?
3. Name two ways music is utilised in religion.
4. What is an *ashiq*? What are the equivalents in Turkey and Yugoslavia?
5. What is the relationship between a singer's melody and the instrumental interludes in an Iranian song?
6. What is *radif*?
7. What are *maqam*, *avaz*, and *dastgah*?
8. What is *darb*? How is it learnt?
9. Classify the instruments discussed into membranophones, chordophones, and aerophones.
10. What pairing of instruments is standardised and used during village festivities? What are the equivalents in Turkey and Yugoslavia?

Iranian musicians playing the *sorna*, *naqqara* and *def*

Turkey

Like folk music in many other societies, some Turkish folk music is used for specific purposes such as weddings and village events. This is demonstrated by the categories into which musicians classify songs:

- *türkü*:   local secular songs
- *sarki*:   urban songs
- *bozlak*:   love songs
- *âgit*:   mourning songs
- *destan*:   ballads and narrative songs. These can be associated with dances, while some dances have their own non-vocal music as well.

Singing, originally done only by men, uses performance conventions such as extremely high pitch and the interpolation of numerous ornaments which give Turkish folk songs their distinctive character. This song, 'Davulcular', has the ornaments written in small notes as it would be performed:

Davulcular

◁ The *kaval*

Ye-di- yĭl - da _____ bir bul - du -ğum _____

Nen - ni gu - zum, _____ nen -ni. _____

2. Nen - ni çal - dĭm _____ sa - de - si - ne _____ iy,

At - lĭm ĭn - mĭş _____ o - da - sĭ - na.

Cĭğ - rĭn _ dyar - cĭn _____ ba - ba -sĭ -na, _____

Nen-ni gör - pen, _____ •• nen - ni , _____

Ye-di yĭl - da _____ bir-bul - du - ğu - m

Nen - ni yav - rum,

'Davulcular' also shows some other features of Turkish song. Notice that the song starts in the upper notes of its scale and that the phrases end on lower notes until the bottom note of the scale is reached (the end notes of the phrases make up a triad). The phrases (the lines of the song) have set numbers of syllables, in this song 8, 8, 8, 6. In Turkish songs these syllable counts are one of the ways in which songs are categorised, and naturally are related to the poetic quality of the texts. Songs are generally considered as being one of two types:

- syllabic: where each syllable of a text is set to one note, or
- melismatic: where a syllable is set to a number of different notes.

Notice the use of melismas in our example (bars 2, 3, 5, 7, etc.).

Dance

Dance is very important in Turkish life. It is not only social but also has religious significance, being part of some rituals. One example of this are the dances performed by the dervishes, who belong to a male religious sect dating from the 13th century which uses dance as a form of religious observance and means of achieving unity with God. Their dance music is based on complex rhythmic and modal formulae involving religious number symbolism.

A village wedding in the 1920s. The dance is accompanied by the *davul* and *zurna*

While in folk songs the rhythm is derived from the words, in dance music there are different conventions. One of these is to subdivide the notes within a bar into uneven smaller units. For example, instead of nine quavers being grouped in three groups of

three, 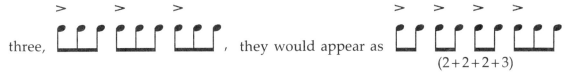 , they would appear as

(2+2+2+3)

which gives four accents, not three. The extra quaver in the last group gives a special effect to Turkish dances which is called 'aksak' (limping), and is also found in dances

of five quaver beats divided as (2+3).

Instruments

Dances are very often accompanied by a pair of instruments, the *davul* (large drum) and *zurna* (a double reed instrument, the reed of which is enclosed in the player's mouth; the player uses circular breathing so the music is uninterrupted). The combination of *davul* and *zurna* is very common: this is demonstrated by the fact that the term '*davul-zurna*' means 'music' in many villages. The presence of a *davul* and a *zurna* is considered obligatory for village festivities.

Turkish wind instruments (L to R): the *zurna*, *kaval*, *mey* and *kaval*. They are accompanied by the *baglama*.

Turkish plucked string instruments: the *tar* (left) and four *baglamas* of different sizes.

♪ Listening

Listen to 'Köylü Düğün Havasi' on the tape. This is performed on the *davul–zurna* combination and shows these instruments in one of their typical uses, a dance tune for a village wedding.

Other instruments include the *baglama* (long-necked lute), the *kaval* and *duduk* (flutes), the *kemence* (three-stringed fiddle), *argul* and *tulum* (bagpipes), the *keman* (European violin), and percussion instruments including the tambourine and different types of drums: *def* (single headed with metal discs attached), *deblek* (single headed frame drum), and *darabak* (single headed goblet drum made of metal or ceramic).

Performance

Performance of songs and dances is usually heterophonic, and Turkish music has a number of different types of scales, some using intervals smaller than Western semitones. Because of this, it is not viable to always try and notate Turkish music on the five line stave. In our example, 'Davulcular', the small arrows above some notes show when notes have been used that do not 'fit' our system of notation. Scales include a heptatonic one often emphasising an augmented second, and modes (Aeolian, Dorian, Ionian, and Mixolydian).

The *baglama*. Compare this Turkish instrument to the Greek *bouzouki* and the Iranian *saz*.

The *kemence*. The body of the instrument is made from a dried gourd.

The *tar*

The *mey*, a single-reed wind instrument

'Davulcular' shows how the ornaments use notes that are not part of the scale in use, but sometimes move around the main melody note by semitone. This song uses the following scale:

This is the Aeolian mode starting on 'g', though the ornaments often use notes not in the scale, and sometimes the e flat is replaced by an e natural (e.g. at the beginning, bars 1–2).

Besides songs and dances, two other important elements of Turkish folk music are the *uzun hava* played by shepherds, and epic songs performed by *asik*. *Uzun hava* (long melody) are semi-improvised solos played on the *kaval* (a 70 to 100 cm long vertical flute). They are based on a remembered store of melodic formulae. The *asik* are renowned poet-musicians who sing or recite epic poems while accompanying themselves on the *baglama*. They are part of a centuries' old tradition that is gradually disappearing.

Questions

1. List the five types of Turkish songs mentioned and define each one.
2. What are two performance conventions of songs?
3. What three typical features of Turkish song can be shown by the song 'Davulcular'?
4. Define the terms 'syllabic' and 'melismatic'.
5. What are 'dervishes'? How do they use dance?
6. a. How are the notes of a bar of nine quavers grouped?
   b. What term refers to this effect?
7. What two instruments are used to accompany dances? Describe each one.
8. List and describe the other instruments discussed.
9. Why is it not possible to always notate Turkish music on a five line stave?
10 a. What modes are specifically mentioned as used in Turkish music?
   b. Which one is the song 'Davulcular' in?
11. a. What are *uzun hava*?
    b. On what are they based?
    c. On what are they played?
12. a. What is an *asik*?
    b. What instrument does he accompany himself with?

Greece

Greek folk music consists of songs and dances that are very often functional, which means they are linked to events such as weddings, funerals, work and religious festivals. It is also highly regionalised, meaning that different regions of the country have their own songs and dances, often referring to local events, people and places. This regionalisation has led to the creation of specific groups of songs and to certain musical qualities being typical of particular areas.

The *kleftic* ballads are an example. These are a collection of songs about the *klefts*, who were mountain-dwelling fighters. They resisted Turkish invaders during the 17th, 18th and 19th centuries. These ballads often describe actual events or are about the lives of the *klefts*, and they belong to the regions along the border between Greece and Turkey.

'Kato Stou Valtou Ta Horia' is a *kleftic* ballad which tells of a letter that was sent to a local bishop warning him of reprisals for his actions in supporting the Turks.

Kato Stou Valtou Ta Horia

Slowly

Ka - to stou Val - tou ta ho - ria____

Ksi - ro - me - ron ke A - gra - fa____

Ke sta pen - de vi - la - e - tia

Fa - te pie - te o - re - a - der - fia.

2. Opou ine i kleftes i poli
   Armatomeni sto flori.
   Kathonte ke tron ke pinoun
   Ke tin Artan foverizoun.

3. Pianoun ke grafoun mia grafi,
   Hezoun ta genia tou Kadi.
   Grafoune ke ston Komboti,
   Proskinoune ton Despoti.

4. "Silogisthite to kala,
   Oti sas keme ta horia.
   Gligora tarmatoliki,
   Oterhomaste san liki."

◁ Dancers accompanied by the violin and *bouzouki* at a wedding celebration in a village tavern

This song uses only one octave for its range, a typical feature of much folk music from the Balkan region. Other musical qualities of regional Greek music are:

- the use of uneven time signatures (e.g. 7/8, 5/8) which also link Greek music to that of neighbouring countries such as Yugoslavia
- the favouring of compound rhythms (e.g. 6/8) in western Greece near Macedonia, showing similarities with Bulgarian music.

'Haralambis' is an example of a Greek dance in 7/8:

Haralambis

ta ne tou - ta   Me   to zo - ri pan-dri - a____

Me   to zo - ri pan-dri - a____   Ti   ka-mo-ma -

ta ne tou - ta   Me   to zo - ri pan-dri - a____

2. Afisate ta logia,
   Ke ta mirologia,
   Kio gero Haralambis
   Den theli pandria.

3. To nou sou, Haralambi,
   Mila pio logika,
   Ke tha se katafero
   Na valis to halka.

This is a dance known as a *Kalamatianos* because it is from the Kalamata region. Notice that although it is a dance, it also has words: singing often accompanies the dancing in Greek music. Also notice that the seven beats of each bar are organised as

3 + 2 + 2, This dance is usually performed at weddings.

The *gaida*

Village musicians with a fiddle and an *oud*

♪ Listening

Listen to 'O Travihtos' on the tape. This is a shuffle dance from the Dodecanese Islands. The instruments are violin accompanied by *lauto* (Greek lute). Notice the use of a drone.

Instruments

The use of instruments is also different throughout the regions of Greece, but overall there are common instruments. These include the *klarino* (a clarinet type instrument), *flogera* (flute), *lauto* (lute), *santori* (dulcimer), *gaida* (bagpipe), and *mandolino*, as well as drums and other percussion.

The best known Greek instrument is the *bouzouki*, a lute-type instrument with eight strings in four sets of pairs. Originally it was a Turkish instrument called the *bozuk saz*, and was brought into Greek music by Turkish refugees in the late 19th and early 20th centuries. Because of its association with Turkish music and a certain type of music called *rembetika*, it has been banned at various times by the Greek government. Along with these Greek instruments, the violin and accordion are also very popular.

Dance

Because of films such as *Zorba the Greek*, most people know that dance is an important part of Greek musical culture. Many Greek dances can be traced back to ancient times: for example, the *hassapiko*, one of the best known dances, was danced by the Greek warriors of Alexander the Great before they went into battle. The *hassapiko* is a line dance

Greek musicians playing *baglamas* (left and right of picture), the guitar, tambourine and *bouzouki*

which follows the direction taken by the person leading. To show he is in charge, he waves a handkerchief with his free hand and invents impromptu steps which the other dancers try to imitate. Some dances start very slowly and gradually accelerate, while others, the *zembekiko* for instance, are danced by a single person in an improvisatory style.

A bouzouki player. Compare the *bouzouki* to the Turkish *baglama*.

Rembetika

Rembetika, or rembetic music, was the music of city-dwelling Greeks from the mid 19th century to the time of the Second World War. It is very different to the regional folk music styles because it grew out of refugee music with much Turkish influence. In the 1920s, continual struggles over territory around the Greek–Turkish border led to a decision to relocate thousands of Greeks and Turks on the basis of religion. Orthodox Turks were sent to live in Greece, Muslim Greeks were sent to Turkey. In Greece this led to the rise of a poor, unemployed subculture in the northern Greek cities and ports, especially Piraeus.

These people brought their music with them, including their instruments such as the *bozuk saz*. The resulting combination of Turkish and Greek music led to the development of a collection of music called *rembetika*, from the slang term '*rembetes*', meaning a small-time thief, drug dealer, or pimp. Rembetic songs were sung in cafe *amans*. The word '*aman*' is Turkish and is an expression of unhappiness. It is very often used melismatically, as the chorus of a rembetic song, and thus for the type of cafe where *rembetika* could be heard.

The words of rembetic songs refer to crime, drugs, death, jails, and unhappy love affairs. Sometimes they are accompanied by homemade instruments, such as the *baglamas*, a small '*bouzouki*' made out of a cigar box or gourd. These instruments were homemade from necessity because the musicians were poor, or were in prison. Rembetic musicians sang folk songs as well as rembetic songs. Here is a folk song that shows the use of the Turkish word '*aman*' as an expression of unhappiness. Notice also the changing time signatures.

Apo Ti Porta Sou Perno

Greek Folk Song

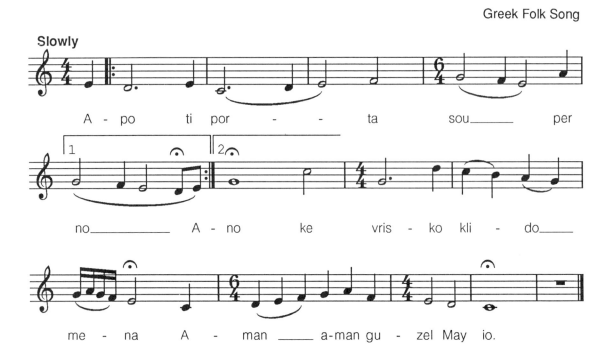

2. Skifto filo ti klidonia,
   Tharro filo esena.
   Aman, aman guzel Mayio!

Questions

1. What sort of social events is Greek music used for?
2. What are *kleftic* ballads?
3. What are *kleftic* ballads about?
4. What musical characteristic of Greek music is shown in the song 'Kato Stou Valtou Ta Horia'?
5. a. What uneven time signatures are often used in Greek music?
   b. Name the type of Greek dance discussed that is in 7/8. How are the quaver beats organised?
6. List the instruments of Greek music, give the equivalent names in English that best describe them, and classify them according to the Sachs–Hornbostel system.
7. What is the best known Greek instrument?
8. What is *rembetika*?
9. How is the word '*aman*' used in rembetic songs?
10. Name a homemade instrument used by rembetic musicians.
11. Name two Greek dances and say how they differ.

This photograph from the 1930s shows *rembetes* and refugees at a cafe *aman*. The instrument on the left is a *saz*.

Yugoslavia

Discussing the music of Yugoslavia is difficult because Yugoslavia is a collection of six republics — Serbia, Croatia, Montenegro, Macedonia, Slovenia, Bosnia–Hercegovina — and two autonomous regions (Vojvodina and Kosovo) with different languages, religions, traditions, and types of music. These differences in music are partly due to the fact that Yugoslavia is between the beginnings of Asia (near Turkey) and the edge of Western Europe, so its range of musical styles fits between the two. In the eastern parts of Serbia, the music has a distinct Turkish flavour, while in the western parts of Croatia and Slovenia it is closer in sound to Austria and Italy. However, it is possible to talk about some common elements in Yugoslavian music — singing styles, dances, the use of certain rhythms, the tradition of the *guslar*, and types of instruments.

Typical of Yugoslavian singing is the use of harmonising parts. This can be seen in the following two examples, one from Macedonia ('Što Mi Omilelo Male') and one from Serbia ('Bolen Leži Mlad Stojan'). In 'Što Mi Omilelo Male', notice the closeness of the parts and that chords are often made up of consecutive notes (e.g. bar 5, c, d, e, g, and bar 6, c, d, e, f#). Notice also the narrow range of the music.

'Bolen Leži Mlad Stojan' shows the use of consecutive thirds.

Bolen Leži Mlad Stojan

Serbian Folk Song

◁ Slovenian dancers accompanied by the *tamburitza*

Macedonian dancers dance to the beat of a drum

Što Mi Omilelo Male

Macedonian Folk Song

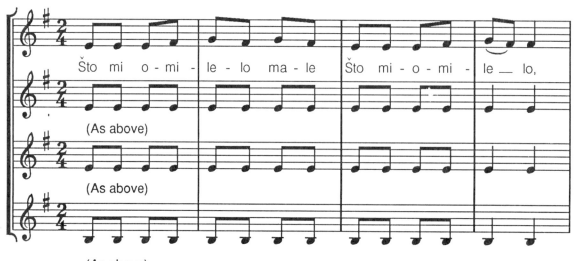

Što mi o - mi - le - lo ma - le   Što mi o - mi - le — lo,

(As above)

(As above)

(As above)

A *kolo* or round dance

Dance

As well as songs, dances are an important part of Yugoslavian music. They are usually group dances performed in a line, not in pairs. The word *kolo* (meaning 'around') is used to refer to dances, and they are usually fast. Here is a dance tune from Macedonia. Notice the use of the time signature of 7/8 grouped as 3 + 2 + 2, and the scale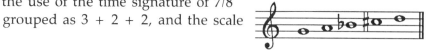

which emphasises the interval of an augmented second, giving the piece an eastern feel.

Dance Tune

Macedonian Dance
Transcribed by P. D. H.

Drum rhythms

The use of such time signatures is one of the best known characteristics of music in the whole Balkan region. These are known as asymmetrical time signatures, that is, they have 5, 7, 9, 11, etc. beats in a bar. Our first song, 'Bolen Leži Mlad Stojan', with its seven quaver beats also organised as 3 + 2 + 2, shows this as well. The use of asymmetrical beats allows the notes in a bar to be grouped in uneven ways, five beats as 2 + 3, seven as 3 + 2 + 2, and nine as either 2 + 3 + 2 + 2, or 2 + 2 + 2 + 3.

Another practice is flexible time signatures, that is, ones that change as the music progresses, as can be seen in this song, 'Oj Vesela, Veselice', also from Serbia:

Oj, Vesela Veselice

Serbian Folk Song

2. Koga god si pogledala,
   svakome si ranu dala.
   I mene si pogledala,
   i meni si ranu dala.

3. Sto bi dala, bijela vilo,
   da me nijesi prije znala?
   Ja bih dala vezen jagluk,
   na jagluku ime moje.

The *guslar*

One of the traditions of Yugoslavian music that is gradually dying out is that of the *guslar*. A *guslar* is a musician, a man who recites extremely long, historical narratives accompanying himself on the one-stringed fiddle, the *gusle*. The narratives are not written down, but must be learnt 'by ear' from another *guslar*. The relationship between the singing, which is highly ornamented in an improvisatory manner, and the accompanying *gusle* part is one of heterophony, as the instrument plays a basic version of the voice's melodic line.

The three-stringed *lirica*, an instrument found in both Macedonia and Dalmatia

A Serbian *gajde* player. Compare the *gajde* to the Greek *gaida*.

Instruments

The instruments used in Yugoslavia are similar to those in other Balkan countries and the Middle East, for example, Iran. Bowed stringed instruments include the *gusle*, and a similar three-stringed fiddle, the *lirica*. Among plucked stringed instruments are the *tamburitza* and the *kanun* (a dulcimer type). Blown instruments include the *sorna* (an oboe type), the *dvojnice* (a double, fipple flute), the *gajde* (bagpipe), *duduk* and *kavall* (endblown flutes). Different types of drums are the *tarabuka* (goblet shaped), *def* (large single headed frame drum), and *goć* (bass drum). As in Turkey and Iran, the combination of *sorna* and *goć* is standardised and considered indispensable for village festivities.

During the early 20th century, Western European instruments — the violin, clarinet, double bass and accordion — were introduced into Yugoslavian music and have now become part of it, either in combination with the original instruments, or in ensembles by themselves.

Music is an important part of village life, and there are large repertoires of songs, dances, and functional pieces to accompany ceremonies and rites, especially weddings and funerals. Accompaniment for songs and dances is often provided by a village group of instrumentalists called a *sazet* (from the Turkish word 'saz', meaning 'instrument') which includes whatever instruments are available.

♪ Listening

Listen on the tape to the example of a Macedonian wedding song sung by a group of men with accompaniment from a *sazet*. Notice the use of a drone, the harmonising in the singing style, the way the verses of the song alternate with instrumental interludes, and the rhythm played on the drum.

A Croatian *tamburitza* ensemble. Notice the different shapes and sizes of the instruments

Questions

1. What is typical of Yugoslavian singing?
2. How do the songs 'Što Mi Omilelo Male' and 'Bolen Leži Mlad Stojan' show different types of harmonisation?
3. a. What does the word '*kolo*' mean?
   b. What is a *kolo*?
   c. How is a *kolo* performed?
4. a. What is meant by 'asymmetrical time signature'?
   b. Which examples did we see with these time signatures?
   c. What time signatures were they?
5. What rhythmic trait can be seen in the song 'O Vesela, Veselice'?
6. a. What is a *guslar*?
   b. What instrument does he use?
   c. Describe this instrument.
7. Is *guslar* music notated? How is it learnt?
8. Three types of chordophones have been discussed in Yugoslavian music. List the instruments under the following headings:
   bowed   lute type   dulcimer type
9. a. Describe the different types of drums discussed.
   b. Which one is paired with the *sorna* as a standard instrumental combination?
10. a. What is a sazet?
    b. Where did the word come from?

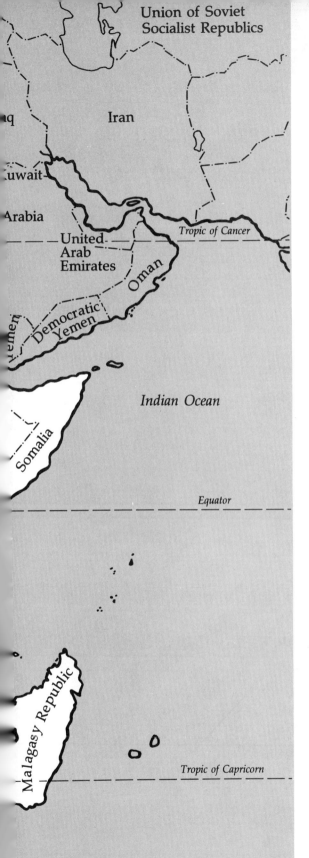

4
AFRICA

The Music of Africa

To discuss the music of all of Africa in the scope of this book is impossible because of the size of the continent, the number of countries it contains, its diversity of ethnic groups and its wide range of musical styles. However, it is possible to look at some overall similarities in African music such as the uses of music and its role in society, and the types of instruments employed. After this general discussion of African music, we will look briefly at music in two areas: Rwanda and Ghana.

The role of music in African society

Music occupies a special place in African society. It is not only used for entertainment, but also accompanies day-to-day activities. It is important in religious ritual and provides a link between daily life and culture. While participation in musical activities involves all members of a society or tribe, especially in singing and dance, there are also specialist trained musicians who are highly valued and who are seen, through their understanding of music, to possess special knowledge. The *griots* of Senegal and other West African countries are an example of this. The word '*griot*' is actually French and was applied to these musicians by French musicologists working in those parts of Africa. Each area has its own term for these musicians: for example, in Gambia they are known as *jali*.

Griots (both men and women) are professional musicians who also have contact, through their music, with the magic/spiritual beliefs of tribes. They fulfil an important role in society by being the bearers of history, legend, accrued wisdom, proverbs, and poetry. In some areas, musicians function within highly organised hierarchies. For example, in Senegal, drummers aspire to the position of master drummer and in Ghana, drummers have a lineage system involving years of learning, and later, passing on their knowledge to others.

◁ Drummers from the Ivory Coast   △ Music is an important part of African life.

In African society music is classified according to its function. There are war songs, planting songs, lullabies, songs to accompany minding cattle, wedding songs and dances, songs for ceremonies such as death rituals, etc. This is one way that music pervades African society and gives everyday life an extra, cultural dimension.

The piece of music which follows, 'Bombo Lao', is an example of a work song from the Congo region. Notice its use of repetition of small melodic/rhythmic motifs and its solo–group call-and-response style.

Bombo Lao

Congo Work Chant

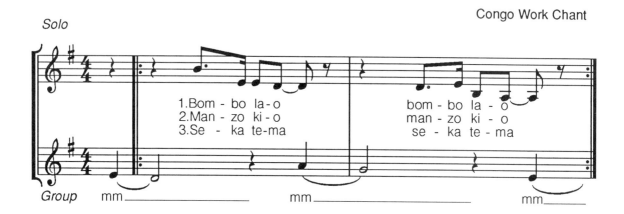

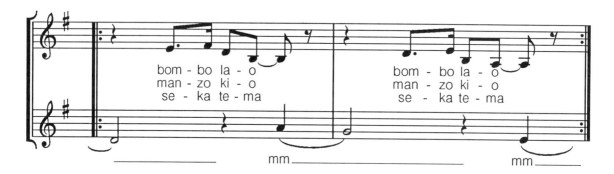

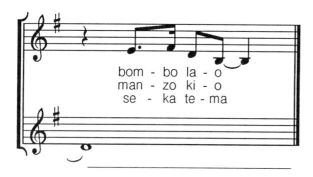

Another way this can be shown is in the transfer of African languages into drum rhythms. Some languages in Africa are tonal, which means that the same syllable can have a number of different meanings depending on its tone or pitch. Certain types of drums (those in the shape of an hourglass, the *tama* in Senegal, *kalengu* in Nigeria and Cameroon, *lunga* in Ghana) can have different pitches determined by the player's control of the skin. These drums are used to imitate the pitches and rhythms of language, so there is a transfer of language into music, and music takes on a role similar to speech.

This is just one way that drums are utilised in African music. Apart from accompanying singing, dancing and rituals, they have a number of other uses. These include being symbols of royalty (for example, in Rwanda), a means of sending messages, a form of poetry recitation, and, through nightlong rituals which centre around drumming performances, a means of preserving and retelling tribal histories and knowledge. In Nigeria, the drum is regarded as a god with holy powers. The range of types of drums in Africa is very large and this is reflected in their method and material of manufacture, the playing styles used, and taboos associated with them.

The significance of drums in African music and society shows us the importance of rhythm as an element of African music. This often involves cross-rhythms, the simultaneous use of different meters, as well as much rhythmic interplay. Other characteristics are the use of recurring beats of irregular patterns, and the use of symmetrical patterns (e.g. ♪ ♪♪ ♪♪). Some of these characteristics can be seen in the following transcription of some of the parts of a complex percussion accompaniment to a dance from Ghana. Notice the simultaneous use of a triple meter (line 3) against ones with a quadruple feel (lines 1 and 2), the importance of syncopation, and the use of a rhythmic motif (♪ ♪· ♪· ♪) which is palindromic.

Drummers from Rwanda

Sovu Dance

Ghanian Dance Tune

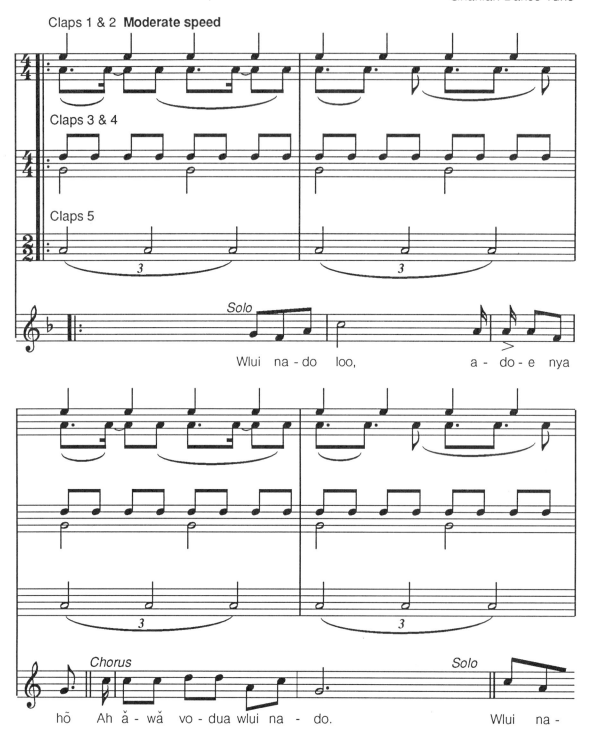

Claps 1 & 2 **Moderate speed**

Claps 3 & 4

Claps 5

Solo

Wlui na - do loo,   a - do - e nya

Chorus   *Solo*

hõ   Ah ă - wă vo - dua wlui na - do.   Wlui na -

do hee, a - do - e nya ho Ah — ă - wǎ vo - dua wlui na-

Chorus

do, a - doe nya hõ. ____

This piece also shows two other important attributes of African music:

- it is pentatonic, using the scale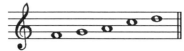

- it uses a call-and-response pattern between a solo singer and a group. Also typical of African music, as this example shows, is the use of small melodic phrases which, in performance, are sung over and over many times. The use of repetition, with added variations, is another characteristic of music from this continent.

Instruments

Drums in Africa come in many shapes and forms: hollow logs, sometimes with a slit along the top and described as 'slit drums'; hourglass shaped (*tama, kalengu*); with rattles attached (e.g. on the Ivory Coast); single and double headed. There are also many different playing styles: some are played with sticks, some by hand, some by a combination of the two.

Listening

Listen to the excerpt of drumming from Rwanda on the tape. Notice how the original meter

$\left[\dfrac{12}{8}\right.$ ♪ | ♩   ♪ ♩   ♪ ♫♫ ♩ $\left.\cdot\right]$ is interrupted by contrasting rhythms shortly after the beginning. This is an example of cross-rhythm — the use of different meters at the same time.

Other percussion instruments include rattles, gourds filled with seeds or stones, bells, sticks and, importantly, handclapping. Types of *balophons* ('xylophones') with keys made from logs or bamboo and both with and without resonators (usually supplied by gourds) are found in nearly all the countries of Africa.

Gourd drums and a *balophon*

The *mbira*.

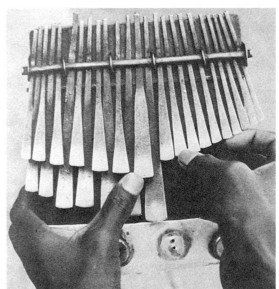

How the *mbira* is played

Other instruments include the *kora* (Senegal area), a large plucked string instrument made from half a gourd with skin stretched over it and described as a harp-lute. There are twenty-one strings attached to a long neck which also has metal rings on it that rattle when the *kora* is played. As well there are types of lutes, harps, zithers, and fiddles. The *jenjili* (Ghana), or *munahi* (Rwanda) is also a string instrument consisting of one string stretched by a bow shaped stick. The sound resonates either in the player's mouth (the strings being plucked sometimes by the teeth, sometimes by hand) or using the chest (the instrument being held against the body), or in a gourd connected to the base of the bow.

Another instrument popular in Central Africa is the *sanza*, also known as the *mbira* (Shona), *likembe* (Rwanda), *agidigbo* and *ubo* (Nigeria). This instrument is uniquely African. It consists of a resonating body (usually a gourd, though a small wooden box is popular as well), above which is attached a soundboard on top of which is a set of keys and added rattles to produce a buzzing when the instrument is played. The size varies greatly and both solo and ensemble playing are found.

♪ Listening

Listen to the *agidigbo* duet from Nigeria on the tape. These are both instruments of the *sanza* type. Notice the use of repetition with variation, the characteristic phrase construction which contrasts a syncopated bar with an unsyncopated one $\left[\begin{smallmatrix}3\\4\end{smallmatrix}\right.$ ♪♩ ♩ ♪♩ ♩ ♩ $\left.\right]$ and the amount of rhythmic complexity in general.

Blown instruments include animal horns, whistles, reed pipes, flute types, and 'trumpets'. All the instruments have different names depending on their country of origin.

Rwanda

In the central African country of Rwanda, vocal and instrumental music are distinct forms. Songs are related to events (e.g. rituals, weddings, etc.), duties (e.g. minding cattle), activities (e.g. hunting), tribal knowledge (history) and so on. The instruments used are *ngoma*, (drums, which symbolise power and were originally exclusive to members of royalty), *munahi* (the musical bow), *likembe*, *inanga* (zither), vertical flutes, horns, fiddles, and 'trumpets'.

The following example is part of a song performed at weddings. Notice the use of call-and-response and that it consists of repetitions of the one phrase with minor variations. The song is accompanied by handclapping, and the call overlaps the end of the response.

The *inanga* from Rwanda

Rwanda Wedding Song

Transcribed by P. D. H.

ah ————:

The *munahi* (Rwanda)

Ghana

Instruments used in Ghana include the fourteen keyed *balophon*, which uses some form of pentatonic scale, the *jenjili* (fiddle), *goonji* (a fiddle made from half a gourd covered with lizard skin and with a single string made from horsehair), *moglo* (a lute type), *zaabia* (gourd rattles), and different types of drums, among them the *gungon*, a large tom-tom with a single snare.

Drums in Ghana sometimes come in a set of sizes which are seen as embodying special relationships. They are referred to as members of a family, the largest being the father, the medium being the mother and the smallest ones, the son and daughter. Drumming is special in Ghanian society and takes years to learn. It embodies history and knowledge of secret topics, and provides the basis for seasonal celebrations. One of these is a twice-yearly drum history during which drumming, song, dance and mime are used in an all-night performance to tell the story of the tribe's past.

The following example, a transcription of only the beginning of a performance, shows several characteristics of African music: it is pentatonic, it involves complex rhythmic interplay and syncopation, it consists of solo–group singing and repetitions of a short melodic phrase. As the performance develops, the instrumental parts — especially the *balophon* — add variations to their basic patterns.

Musicians play the *balophon*, drum and harp

Tu Tu Le Tu

Ghanian Folk Tune
Transcribed by P. D. H.

Bell (high)
Rattle

Drum
Bell (low)

Balophon

Solo

N   saa   be so zie   ke yel   ___   ke re win-aa   yir

Questions

1. Apart from entertainment, what are some other uses of music in Africa?
2. Name some of the specific activities which African music accompanies.
3. What are *griots*? Where are they from?
4. Explain the concept of language transferred to drum rhythms.
5. List the ways drums are used in Africa.
6. What is cross-rhythm?
7. What is typically African about the rhythm of the Sovu dance?
8. 'Sovu dance' is pentatonic and uses call-and-response. Define these two terms.
9. Classify the following instruments according to the Sachs–Hornbostel classification system and define each one: *balophon*, *kora*, *kalengu*, *jenjili*, *sanza*, *inanga*.
10. Which three musical characteristics of the Rwanda wedding song are typical of African music?
11. What is typical about the piece from Ghana, 'Tu Tu Le Tu'?

Kora players from Senegal

These buskers use a variety of homemade instruments for their performance

Double metal bells and a tall drum

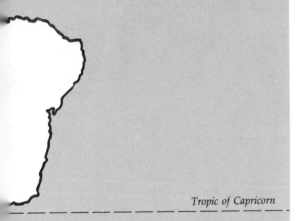

Tropic of Cancer

ʒo

ana

Equator

Tropic of Capricorn

Atlantic Ocean

5

SOUTH
America
and the
CARIBBEAN

The Music of South America

Folk music in South America is very varied. This is understandable when we consider that we are talking about a whole sub-continent made up of thirteen countries, and these countries show the influences of different cultures and invasions. For the purpose of trying to classify the music of South America, we can divide the countries into two areas:

- the Andean countries, which follow the Andes mountain chain down the western side of South America — Peru, Bolivia, Chile, Argentina
- Brazil.

Music of the Andean area developed out of the ancient traditions of the Aztecs and Incas while Brazil's music is a mixture of indigenous Brazilian Indian music, African music and European music. The European influences in both these areas differ as well, depending on which country colonised them. The Andean countries have the influence of Spanish music, while Brazil's music is influenced by that of Portugal.

Andean Music

Ancient Aztec and Inca drawings often depict instruments being used to accompany religious rituals. From these drawings we know that instruments were played in groups and that the Aztecs used drums, flutes, conch shell 'trumpets', and rattles, while the Incas had drums, panpipes, and ocarinas. Of these, the flutes are of two types: end-blown (like the recorder) and side-blown (like the modern concert flute), while the panpipes are made of either pottery or cane and exist in a number of sizes up to five feet in length.

◁ A Peruvian endblown flute   △ Conch shell 'trumpets'

The panpipes are perhaps the best known instrument from South America, but few people know of the intricate way in which they are played. They are often played in pairs, with the two players using complicated rhythms that fit together. The result sounds as though one person is playing very rapidly. An example of this can be seen in the following piece (bars 8 and 9), where the two melodic lines have syncopated rhythms that complement each other:

Yaku Kantu

Bolivian Circle Dance
Transcribed by P. D. H.

Notice also the use of the rhythm ♪♩ ♪, which is typical of South American music.

Flutes and panpipes are often used in conjunction with various string instruments, which were unknown in South America before the arrival of Europeans in the 16th century. These string instruments include:

- *charango*: a small, high pitched imitation guitar made from the shell of an armadillo
- *cuatro*: another small guitar, this one with only four strings
- *tiple*: a three-stringed guitar, or one having three sets of double strings
- *guitarrone*: a large four-stringed guitar which is tuned as for the double bass and plays the bass line.

Charango players.

'Zamponeando' is a dance tune from Peru. It would be played on panpipes and a *bombo*.

Zamponeando

Peruvian Folk Tune
Transcribed by P. D. H.

* *Bombo* (dull bass drum), *charango* and a bass line start at B

Bombo rhythm

Just as the *charango* is made from part of an animal, the *quena*, an endblown flute, is made from the legbone of a llama, and in ancient times is known to have been made from human bones.

Drums and other percussion instruments, including rattles made from gourds, are very important in Andean music. The drums, such as the Argentinian *bombo*, often have heads made from unshaven sheepskin which results in a dull sound rather than the open, ringing drum sound heard in European music. This dull drum beat is one of the distinctive sounds of Andean music. Unlike European drums, the *bombo* is played both on the head, or skin, and at the same time by the player's other hand, on the body of the drum, often in a syncopated or contrasting rhythm. A rhythmic practice used on the *bombo* is the playing of two rhythms simultaneously, which is called polyrhythm. For example:

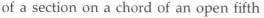

The songs and dances of this region are often pentatonic, or have a strong pentatonic feel. For instance, our Bolivian panpipe melody, 'Yaku Kantu', is pentatonic except for the four times an 'A' appears. They also use repetition to build one or two short melodies into a whole piece. Sometimes these repetitions get faster and faster, or include the addition of new percussion parts. The use of repetition can be demonstrated in our first example which is used to accompany a dance that can last for hours: the musicians simply play the two melodies, over and over, alternately.

'Yaku Kantu' also demonstrates another characteristic of Andean music: the ending of a section on a chord of an open fifth

Panpipes and drums

This is another distinctive sound you will start to recognise as you listen to more South American music. Notice the use of a common motif to end both sections of melody. This is also demonstrated in parts of our second example, 'Zamponeando'.

♪ Listening

Listen to 'Totoras' on the tape. This piece is from Peru and demonstrates panpipes, *charango*, and *bombo*. Notice the use of contrasting speeds and repetition. Compare it to both 'Yaku Kantu' and 'Zamponeando'.

The influence of European music is not only evident in the creation of new instruments such as the *charango* — which obviously imitates the Spanish guitar — but also in the way that original native instruments, such as the panpipes, are tuned. Traditional methods have changed to those of European music, so it is possible to play European style music on instruments that are originally from another tradition. This can also be seen in the way that Andean music is sometimes arranged in the style of European folk music, with accompanying chords and a bass part.

A side-blown Andean flute

Berimbas and tambourines accompany a dance

Brazil

Like the music of South America in general, Brazilian music is very diverse. This diversity is partly due to the three types of music that have been combined to make up Brazilian music. These are the music of the original South American Indians, the music of the Portuguese colonisers, and the music of slaves brought from Africa between the 16th and 19th centuries.

The contribution of the original Indians can be seen in the continued use of instruments such as flutes and various percussion instruments, and in the links between singing and dancing. The influence of Portuguese music is evident in the use of European style harmony and melodies, and in the popularity of string instruments which, as mentioned previously, were not known in South America before the arrival of the Europeans. These string instruments include the harp (which in a smaller form than the European concert harp is very popular among folk musicians), various forms of the violin, and different types of guitar such as the *cavaquinho*, a small four-stringed guitar sounding similar to the Andean *charango*. Another Portuguese influence is the use of the ambiguity between 6/8 and 3/4 time signatures.

By far the most distinctive characteristics of Brazilian folk music can be traced to the music brought from Africa by slaves. During the period of slavery (16th–19th centuries) approximately four million slaves were taken from West Africa to South America, the majority of them to Brazil. As occurred in America and Jamaica, the slaves 'carried' their music and instruments with them, so in Brazil we can trace musical elements that are African in origin. These include the importance of rhythm as the main element of music, which can be seen in the prominence given to dance music and the wide use of drums and other percussion instruments. Often the names of drums and dances reflect African

Musicians and dancers in fancy dress for Carnival celebrations, Rio de Janeiro, Brazil

words: for example, the pair of drums called *congas*, and the dance called the *conga*, remind us of their origins in the Congo region of Africa. Also in common with African music is the practice of using 'non–musical' things as instruments: for example, boxes, cans, pots and pans. As is found in African music, rhythmic effects such as polyrhythm and syncopation are very important.

Another African trait is the social importance given to dance. Brazilian dances are well known throughout the world and include the *maxixe* and *merengue*, as well as the most famous, the *samba*. The *samba* was originally an African dance called the *lundo*, and has the characteristic rhythm. It is so important among Brazilians that for the Mardi Gras carnival each year, they go to special locally-run *samba* schools to practise it. Here is the music of a *samba de morro* (a *samba* from the hills rather than the city) with accompanying percussion parts. Notice the use of highly syncopated rhythms.

Samba de Morro

Brazilian Dance Tune

Accompanying percussion:

Instruments used in Brazil that can be traced directly to Africa include the *berimba*, or musical bow, different types of drums, and whistles. Other Brazilian instruments include the *afoxe* (a gourd with strings of beads over its surface), the *chocalho* (a bell), the *reco-reco* (a piece of bamboo that is serrated and scraped), the *maracas*, *claves*, *cabasa*, and *agogo* (two bells connected by a loop and hit with a drumstick).

As well as songs and dances, Brazilian popular music includes the *choro*. Originally the *choro* was a collection of European dances, such as the waltz and tango, played by a group of instrumentalists with Brazilian rhythms and 'flavour' added. Eventually this type of music came to include singing and, later, any type of solo instrumental piece of a typically Brazilian style.

Questions

1. Why is South American folk music so varied?
2. What are the two main geographic divisions made when discussing South American music?
3. a. Where is Spanish influence strong?
   b. Where is Portuguese influence strong?
4. a. What instruments were used by the Aztecs?
   b. What instruments were used by the Incas?
5. Describe the way pairs of panpipes perform together.
6. List the string instruments used in Andean music and describe each one.
7. What is a *quena* and what is it made from?
8. What is a *bombo* and what two unusual characteristics does it have?
9. a. What three cultures contributed to Brazilian music?
   b. What did each culture contribute?
10. What rhythmic effects are important in Brazilian music?
11. a. List three Brazilian dances.
    b. Which is the most famous?
12. What is a modern *choro*?
13. List all the instruments mentioned as being used in South American music under the following headings:
    Strings   Winds   Percussion   Other

The Music of the Caribbean

The islands of the Caribbean comprise a diverse collection of nations and cultures, each with its own distinctive music. However, because of historical events such as European colonisation and slavery, they have similarities that enable us to group them together. These similarities include instruments. Throughout this region the guitar, in a number of different sizes, is popular, and percussion instruments such as *berimba*, *claves*, *maracas*, *cabasa*, *reco-reco*, and *agogo* are found, as well as many types of drums, especially *congas* and their smaller version, *bongos*. There is also the practice of using non-musical things as instruments, including bottles hit with spoons, different sizes of frying pans, saucepan lids, boxes, and petrol drums. One of the most important in this group is the *quinto*, a wooden box developed from African slit drums. As well there are wooden and bamboo flutes.

The introduction of the guitar, and stringed instruments in general, to this region is due to its colonisation, and especially to the influence of Spanish and Portuguese music. As in the countries of South America, the guitar exists in a number of sizes, including the *guitarrone* (a large four-stringed bass guitar tuned an octave below the bottom strings of the guitar), the *tres* (a small guitar with three sets of double strings) and the *cuatro* (small with four strings). The banjo, in various sizes and numbers of strings, is also popular.

One of the most important facts about music in the Caribbean region is that it shows the influences of music from a number of other countries, especially African and European. European music of the colonising powers (England, Spain, Portugal, Holland and France) has mainly contributed Western style harmony to the music of this area. The influence of African music (brought from Africa by slaves between the 16th and 19th centuries) can be seen in a number of ways, including the use and naming of instruments. Often Caribbean instruments are called by names that show a direct link with African ones: for example, in Jamaica pairs of long cylindrical drums are known as *'aprinting'* (in the African language Twi, *'oprenteng'*), a small drum is called a 'repeater' after the African drum a *'peta'*, and an instrument made from a cowhorn is called an *'abeng'*, the name still used in Ghana for instruments made from animal horns. As well, terms referring to music and musical events can be traced to Africa: the *mambo*, a Cuban dance, reminds us of the Bantu word *'mambe'* which means 'song', and the name given to religious observances involving music in Jamaica, *'kumina'*, could have been derived from the Central African term *'kumu'* which implies playing an instrument, as well as melody and rhythm.

The African influence in Caribbean music can also be seen in dance steps, religious celebrations, and the distinctive rhythms of dances. Dances are a very important part of the music of this region, and often there is no distinction between song and dance. Some of the original folk dances (for example the Cuban *rumba*) have been developed by commercial musicians so that often people don't realise their origins.

Some of the countries of this area have musical traditions that can be discussed separately. These include Jamaica (*mento*, work songs, and *kromanti* and *kumina*), Trinidad (calypso and steel-band music), and Cuba (dance styles and song).

◁ Carnival musicians with steel drums, Trinidad

Musicians accompany dancers on a drum and box

Jamaica

Two types of music in Jamaica are *mento* and work songs. *Mento* is sometimes used to refer to Jamaican folk music as a whole. It is a hard term to define as it seems to include different types of songs and dances, and the combinations of instruments on which they are performed, ranging from harmonica accompanied by rattles, to bands of banjo, guitar, rumba-box (a large *sanza* with a few plucked metal tongues), and percussion, with modern Western instruments — violin, trumpet, saxophone — added if necessary. What is typical of *mento* performances is the use of offbeat guitar accompaniment, a prominent bass line, and melodic improvisation around well known tunes. The following example is a transcription of part of a *mento* group's version of 'Linstead Market'. The tune is played first, followed by a variation. Notice how the conflicting rhythms give it a sense of improvisation.

Linstead Market

Instrumental Version
Transcribed by P. D. H.

Notice also the use of simple harmony (chords I, IV, V, and ii) and that it is based on repetition of two chord patterns: G – C – G – D7 – G, and G – Am – D7 – G). These are common features of harmony in the Caribbean area and can be seen in such popular songs as 'Jamaica Farewell', 'The Peanut Vendor', 'Matilda', and 'Mango Walk'.

♪ Listening

Listen to 'Oh Carolina' on the tape. This is an example of *mento* and the instruments are banjo, guitar, repeater, *maracas* and rumba box (bass *sanza*).

Due to the popularity of modernised versions of songs such as the 'Banana Boat Song' ('Day-oh, day-oh, daylight come an' me wanna go home'), work songs are well known as typical of Jamaican music. They usually employ a call-and-response pattern between a soloist and the rest of the singers and, as their name suggests, were originally sung while working. We know from written records that they were sung by slaves. Notice

Musicians playing *maracas* and drums. Notice two of the drums are made from barrels.

in the following example the use of a pentatonic scale and the repeated response ('Hill an' gully').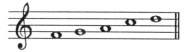

Hill an' Gully Rider

Jamaican Traditional Song

Hill an' gul-ly rid - er, hill an' gul-ly,

hill an' gul-ly rid - er, hill an' gul-ly, an' a

been dung low dung, hill an' gul-ly, an' a

low dung an' bes-sy dung, hill an' gul-ly, An' ya

bet' min tum-ble dung, hill an' gul-ly.

The use of these two devices (pentatony and call-and-response) is often seen as linking these songs to some original African music. Another feature of this song is the use of the rhythm which is found throughout the whole Caribbean region.

Kromanti and *kumina* are two types of Jamaican music that belong to the descendants of African slaves. These descendants are referred to as the 'Bongo Nation'. Both *kromanti* and *kumina* are religious observances involving drumming, singing and dance. *Kromanti* belongs to the descendants of the Maroons, slaves who escaped and fled to live in the mountains in the east of Jamaica. *Kumina* belongs to the descendants of 'voluntary' African labourers brought to Jamaica in the mid 19th century.

Both *kromanti* and *kumina* involve nightlong musical rituals associated with African ancestor spirit possession. In the view of both musicologists and practitioners, they represent a close link between Jamaican and African music. This link can be seen not only in the use of African words and phrases in the singing and naming of instruments, but in the drum rhythms and performance style which involve rhythmic improvisation over repeated patterns for the drummers, and long passages of solo–chorus call-and-response for the singers.

♪ Listening

Listen to 'Mandumbe' on the tape. This is an excerpt from a *kumina* ceremony. Notice the call-and-response, use of repetition, and the accompanying drum and percussion rhythms. Compare this to the taped excerpts in the African section of this book.

Jamaican dancers

A marching steel band from Trinidad

Trinidad

Calypso is a type of Trinidadian folk music that has important social implications. It is not only a sung form of folk music, but its texts, which in some songs are often improvised, can be a type of satire and social comment. Besides satirical calypso songs, there are also ones that are simply humorous. Calypso dates from the early 19th century and has often used call-and-response between a soloist (who invents the topical text) and the listeners (who sing a stock response). Melodic originality is not the point of calypso, tunes being recycled when needed. Once the pattern of solo–group has been established, percussion instruments join in as accompaniment. During the 1950s and 1960s, commercialised versions of calypso songs and composed songs in calypso style became very popular.

The following example is a humorous composed song in calypso style. It shows the use of simple harmonic progressions, and rhythms typical of Caribbean songs:

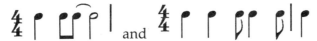

Too Much Coffee In De Coffee Pot

by Ray Rivera and Harry Stride

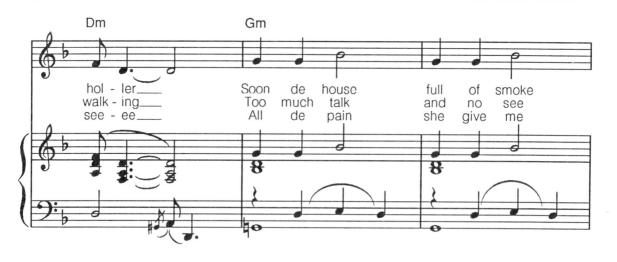

hol - ler___ Soon de house full of smoke
walk - ing___ Too much talk and no see
see - ee___ All de pain she give me

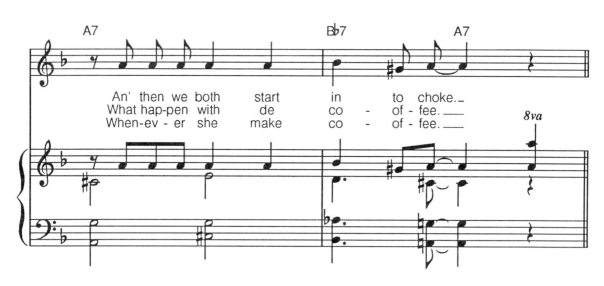

An' then we both start in to choke.___
What hap-pen with de co - of - fee.___
When-ev - er she make co - of - fee.___

8va

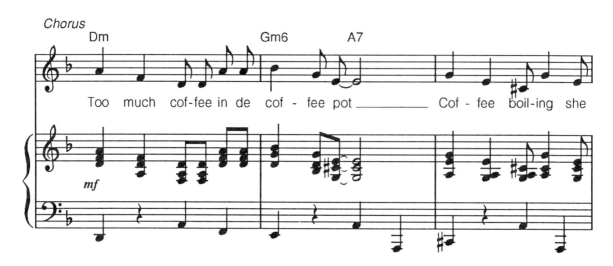

Chorus

Too much cof-fee in de cof - fee pot _____ Cof - fee boil-ing she

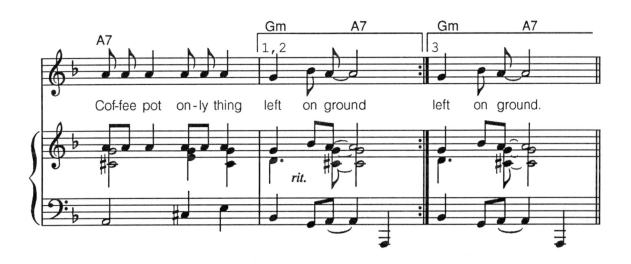

While calypso songs can be performed at any time, they are particularly associated with Carnival (held during the weeks before Easter) and are an important part of the celebrations.

Steel bands and their music are well known elements of Trinidadian music. The instruments that make up a steel band are made from petrol drums. This practice started after the Second World War, using fuel containers that the American forces, who had used Trinidad as a fuelling base in the Caribbean, had left behind. Originally these instruments were played by poor people who could not afford 'real' instruments, but eventually they became popular and bands are often sponsored by large companies whose names they adopt: for example, the Colgate-Palmolive Melodians, and the ICI All Stars. The range of music played by steel bands is wide, from calypso and other folk tunes, to arrangements of classical music.

A pan, the common name for a steel drum, is made by cutting the top section off a petrol drum, different depths making different pitch ranges. The pan is tuned by beating sections of its top, or lid, to thin the metal. Pans are made in four sizes called ping-pong, guitar, cello, and bass (smallest/highest to largest/lowest). Untuned rhythmic accompaniment is often added on brake-drum hubs. The following transcription is the opening sections of a piece of Trinidadian steel band music. Notice the repetitive bass rhythm, the use of simple harmony (a typical feature of music in the Caribbean and seen already in 'Linstead Market'), and that the second section (bars 19–34) is a variation of the first section. This piece uses the rhythms 𝄴 ♩· ♩· ♩ , 𝄴 ♩ ♫ ♫ and 𝄴 ♫ ♫ which are typical of Caribbean music. These rhythms, like those in 'Hill an' Gully Rider' use the device of syncopation.

Tamboo bamboo, bamboo 'drums', were popular before the development of steel drums. In the 1920s large *tamboo bamboo* bands were banned because of bamboo stick fights between bands.

Somebody Whisper To Me

Trinidad Steel Band
Transcribed and edited by P. D. H.

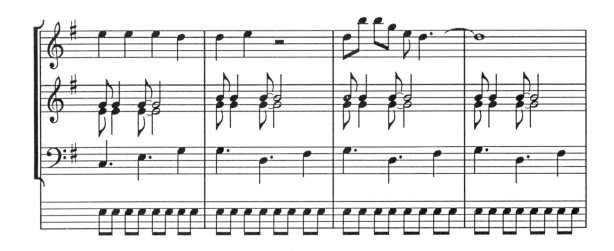

D.C. al fine

Drums play an important part in Cuban music and dance

Cuba

An important component of Cuban music is the large number of dance forms, some of which have become standard, commercialised 'Latin American' dances. What makes each dance distinct is its use of an accepted underlying rhythm. Some of these are:

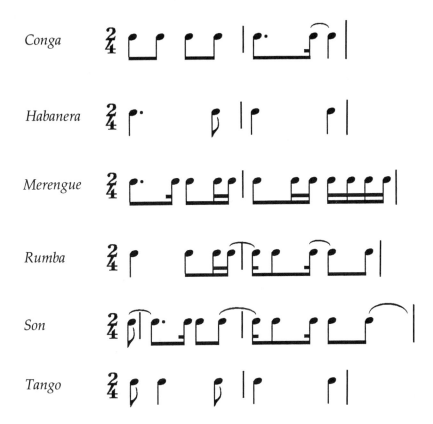

Of these, the *habanera* reminds us of its Cuban heritage (the capital of Cuba is Havana), and the *conga* of an African link (the Congo is one of the areas in Africa from which slaves were taken). The *tango* is often thought of as Argentinian but is found throughout the Caribbean as well, and the *rumba*, which today is considered as one dance, originally referred to a type of dancing and singing in which mime played a role. The accompaniment to these original *rumbas* was provided by a percussion ensemble in which a lead drummer improvised changing rhythms over the accepted rhythmic accompaniment.

Our last example of Caribbean music is a Cuban song, 'Guantanamera'. This song is popular not only in Cuba but throughout the whole region, where it has the status of an unofficial anthem. It shows, like the other examples of Caribbean music discussed, the use of simple harmony (chords I, IV, and V7), and (except for bars 13 and 14) a chordal ostinato (D – G – A7).

Guantanamera

Cuban Traditional Song

Questions

1. a. List the instruments commonly used throughout the Caribbean.
   b. What type of instrument is most prevalent?
2. Name two ways in which the influence of European music is shown in the music of this region.
3. How can the influence of African music be demonstrated?
4. a. What is *mento*?
   b. What is typical of *mento*?
5. What two harmonic features of 'Linstead Market' are also typical of music in the Caribbean area?
6. What two musical features of work songs are seen as links with African music?
7. a. What are *kromanti* and *kumina*
   b. How are their links with African music shown?
8. a. What is calypso?
   b. What are two types of calypso songs?
9. a. Explain the manufacture of a Trinidadian steel drum.
   b. What are the names of the sizes of steel drums from highest to lowest?
   c. What untuned percussion is sometimes added to a steel band?
10. a. The musical examples in this section use a number of rhythms which give the music a Caribbean flavour. List four of these rhythms.
    b. What musical feature do they all show?
11. What musical feature is used to define the different Cuban dance styles?
12. What two musical features of 'Guantanamera' are also typical of the other examples of Caribbean music discussed?

2. Mi verso es de un verde claro
   Y de un carmín encendido. (Rpt).
   Mi verso es un ciervo herido,
   Que en le monte busca amparo,

Chorus
Guantanamera, etc.

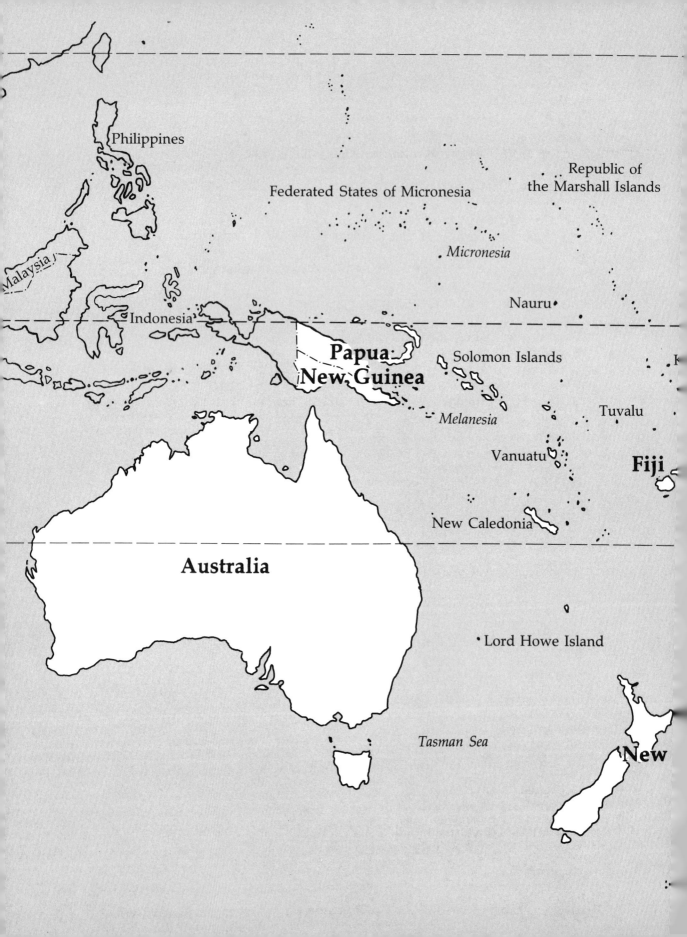

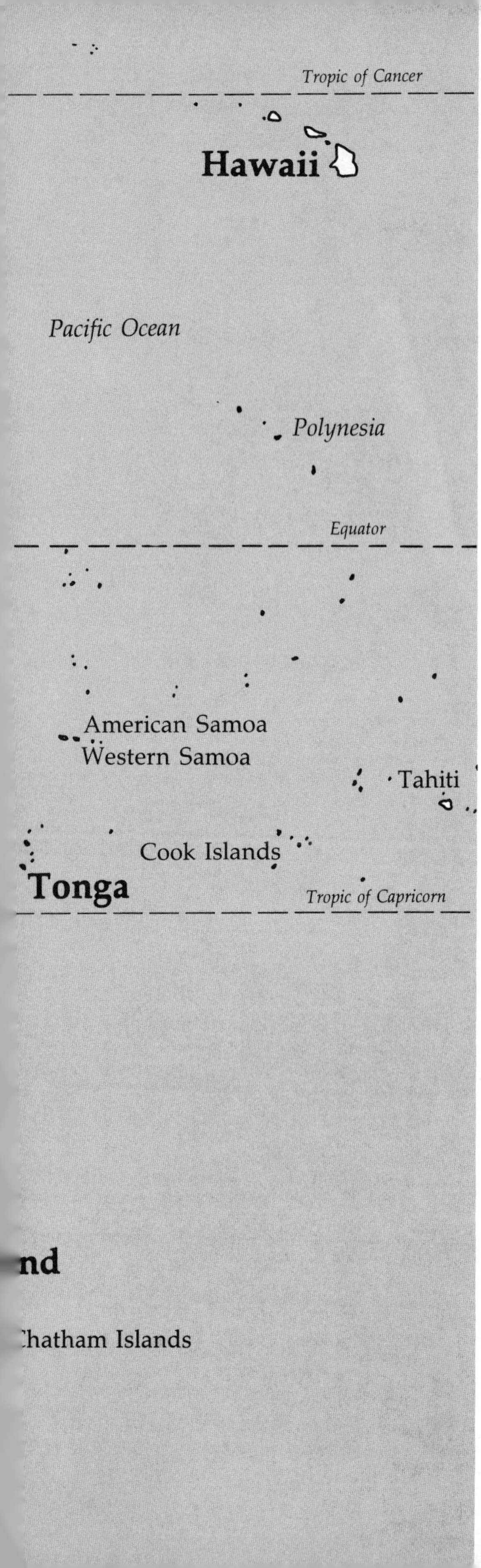

Tropic of Cancer

Hawaii

Pacific Ocean

Polynesia

Equator

American Samoa
Western Samoa

Tahiti

Cook Islands

Tonga
Tropic of Capricorn

nd

Chatham Islands

6

The

PACIFIC

Region

Polynesian Music

The islands of Polynesia form a rough triangle bounded by Hawaii in the north, Easter Island in the south-east and New Zealand in the south-west.

Ancestors of the present-day Polynesians originated in Asia and arrived in Polynesia from Melanesia around three thousand years ago, settling first in Tonga. The Polynesians were great navigators and seafarers and eventually inhabited all the islands of Polynesia, creating throughout the Pacific a social structure based on a rigid caste system, cultural links and musical similarities.

Society throughout Polynesia was organised into a stable structure based on rank and maintained through various taboos and rituals. The most important chiefs were identified as gods. Much of the traditional music of Polynesia is concerned with religious rites, honouring the gods and chiefs and reinforcing the kin-groupings.

Music throughout Polynesia is classified according to the role it plays in tribal life (function) and the way it is performed (style).

The text or the poetry is the most important aspect of Polynesian music. Melody, rhythm and dance are of secondary importance and mainly decorative in role.

♪ Listening

'Sasa' is a vigorous war dance accompanied by slit drums, rattle, slapping of body, foot stamping and handclapping. As you listen, notice how voices are used as instruments.

A comparison of Tongan (Western Polynesian) and Hawaiian (Eastern Polynesian) music illustrates the similarities of music found across thousands of miles of ocean.

Tonga

Tonga was the first of the Polynesian islands to be settled, Hawaii the last. Tongan music, like all Polynesian music, is based primarily on poetry or text, enhanced by the addition of melody and movement (dance). Percussion instruments of various kinds are also used as accompaniment.

The melody is made up of only a few notes of narrow range. The main melody line (*fasi*) is often accompanied by a second, lower melody (the *laulalo*, or drone). Both are sung by men. Additional parts which decorate the melody can be provided by other males or females. With the arrival of the missionaries in the Pacific, this formal structure was easily adapted to hymn-singing, being something similar to Western four-part harmony.

The most elaborate songs in terms of both melody and number of parts are those performed for important ceremonial purposes. These are called *faiva* and they can have as many as one hundred performers, singing in parts and performing various choreographed movements and actions, accompanied by drums and other instruments.

The history of a tribal chief, his ancestors, interrelationships through marriage and other important events are formed into long recited narratives. Because of the importance of maintaining this oral history without change, errors in performance are guarded against by strict performance codes and taboos.

◁ Tongan girls take part in a standing dance.

Work songs, game songs, funeral songs and songs used for celebrations are other kinds of music. These songs are generally built on short two line texts, often performed as a call-and-response. The rhythms of most songs are governed by the words and the melodic range is quite narrow. Part-singing produces a kind of heterophonic texture.

Listening

Listen to 'Lamagaffe' on the tape. This song, about an octopus and a rat, shows typical Polynesian harmonisation.

Songs which accompany death can be of two types:

• those which are emotional in content. They are usually sung on one note, a mournful dirge interspersed with wails.
• those which are formalised songs of grief with richer poetic content, more melodic decoration and more complex part singing.

Hand gestures are an important part of Tongan dances

Singers accompany themselves on guitars and banjo.

Work songs (*tau'a'alo*) are much simpler in both the text and the melodic decoration, while children's songs are the simplest, usually quite short and using only a few notes. Some songs, like war dances, are only performed by men, while others are women-only performances. Gospel chanting (*tarava*) is also a popular song form in Tonga today.

Dance is an important adjunct to some types of music and is classified into sitting and standing dances. The *ula* is perhaps the most famous of the standing dances, with expressive gestures made by the arms together with head movements. The legs do not move much. This dance, performed by a group of women, is accompanied by a song made up of only one or two short repeated phrases, and using only a few notes. Idiophones such as a drum or bamboo sticks provide an accelerating tempo. In the male equivalent, the feet stay together and the knees are waggled rhythmically.

Other Tongan dances include the *me'elaaufola*, a group dance accompanied by stamping tubes, and the *lakalaka*. This is a modern standing dance, based on a traditional one. It combines part-singing and choreographed movements. Canonic effects, syncopations and improvisations are created within the group. Performance in Tongan music becomes more complex with the addition of more parts. A large performance can be made up of more than one hundred people singing (in a number of parts), performing (a number of movements), and accompanying (on a number of instruments). The group attempts to put all these elements together into a precise and overall effective performance.

Instruments include slit drums, bamboo stamping tubes, and sounding boards. Stamping tubes are made of hollow wood or bamboo. They are 'drum equivalents' and make a percussive sound when hit together or on the ground. Handclapping is frequently used. Bell stones (large stones that produce a resonant ring) were ancient instruments used for important ceremonial and religious purposes. The *fangufangu* (a nose flute which plays a small four note scale), conch shell trumpets and panpipes are the most used aerophones. Many Western instruments such as the guitar, ukelele and banjo have been adopted by the Tongans and are now used to play or accompany traditional music. This adaptation of external European culture into the traditional Polynesian one has also occurred with the use of Western melodies and harmonies in the performance of traditional songs. This process is called acculturation.

The *hula ipu* is made from gourds and is used either as a drum or a stamping tube

Hawaii

Hawaii was the last of the islands of Polynesia to be settled. Though more than 6000 kilometres from the closest large islands in Polynesia, the music is similar.

Originally performances of traditional music were only given by priests and professionals trained in music schools supported by tribal chiefs. Their role after training was to provide entertainment for their masters. Hawaiian music — both song and dance — was performed by small groups of trained performers, each individual performer being skilled in a variety of instruments and elaborate dance movements.

As in Tonga, traditional Hawaiian music is a combination of poetic text, simple melodic lines, rhythms and movement — text being the most important element. Music performs many functions, from simple learning chants of children, to work songs, songs for entertainment, to important religious and ceremonial songs.

The poetic text (*mele*) is made up of melodies of small range and few notes. The words are usually in an isometric pattern which is repeated with small rhythmic changes, and frequently accompanied by interpretative movements (*hula*). The combination of song with dance is called *mele hula*. The movements of the Hawaiian *hula* are more fluid than the Tongan *ula*, with the addition of swaying hips and more variation in the leg and arm movements.

In 'A Hilo Au', the Hawaiian song that follows, notice the use of only three tones (a three note scale). The melody is made up of two short motifs, one consisting of a downward leap (a to e) and the other moving upward and back by step (a-b-a). The two patterns alternate throughout the song. The rhythm varies around these two melodic cells.

A Hilo Au

Hula
Transcribed by Elizabeth Tatar

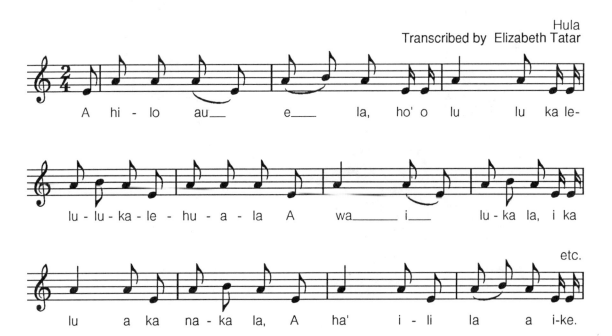

Indigenous instruments are more varied in Hawaii than in any other part of Polynesia. They include membranophones made from wood or coconut shells with sharkskin heads, called *pahu*; a large and diverse collection of idiophones such as slit drums (wooden trunks with a large cut on the upper side), rhythm sticks, bamboo stamping tubes, and rattles made of bamboo and seed pods (*uliuli*); and aerophones including mouth flutes, nose flutes, and mouth bows. Clapping and body percussion are the most common rhythmic accompaniment. With acculturation, string instruments such as the ukelele have been adopted to accompany traditional music.

Some song and song/dances include:

- *Ko'ihonua* (*mele inoa*): long, often extremely long, narratives based on the history and genealogy of the ruling chiefs. They are remembered and have to be recited without error or alteration. This is done by reciting the narrative rhythmically. *Ko'ihonua* are performed quickly and are often accompanied by choreographed movements and percussion instruments.

- *Kanikau*: songs associated with death. They are of two kinds: spontaneous outpourings of grief interspersed with wailing and mournful cries; and more stylised and decorative songs to do with paying homage to the deceased.

The *uliuli*, a Hawaiian rattle made from seed pods

Questions

1. What were the first and last islands settled in Polynesia?
2. What is the most important element in Polynesian music?
3. What is meant by style and function when referring to music?
4. Describe three stylistic features of Tongan music.
5. a. What is the most famous Tongan standing dance?
   b. What are its musical features?
6. What is meant by acculturation?
7. a. What is a *mele hula*?
   b. How does it differ from its Tongan equivalent?
8. What are *fasi* and *laulalo*?
9. What is *tarava*?
10. Give these instruments a Sachs–Hornbostel classification:
    uliuli, *pahu*, *fangufangu* and ukelele

The *hula*

Fiji

There are more than three hundred islands making up the country we know as Fiji, and the population is comprised of Indians, Chinese, Europeans and Pacific Islanders. The indigenous Fijians are of Melanesian descent however their music and culture is closer to that of Polynesia. The traditional music of Fiji is closely related to that of Tonga and the instruments are also similar, reflecting their common ancestry. Musical styles vary between islands and there is also a difference between the classical or traditional music-chants and that of the missionary-influenced songs.

As in the rest of the region, the voice is the main instrument in Fijian music. The words and the text are important rather than the melody. The words of some songs, especially those used in events of important social significance such as formalised funeral ceremonies, are not allowed to be changed or altered. Once they have been forgotten, other words cannot be substituted. That is why some traditional Fijian songs have gaps in them, and the words are occasionally uneven. Traditionally, music composition belonged only to certain people. They alone were allowed to create the words of the text, add the movements and teach it.

The pitch range of songs is quite narrow and many melodies are often sung around or on only the one note. Other melodies might be made up of a few notes, but generally not more than four. When melodies were made up using these scales, the notes used were generally the note four tones below the starting note and the note a second above (what Western musicians call the tonic, dominant and supertonic). The overall effect is of a monotone. A chant demonstrating this can be seen in the piece 'A Hilo Au' from Hawaii, which is representative of the Polynesian style.

The words to most Fijian music are divided into verses, and the ends to songs are often marked by a downward slide or glissando. Dynamics don't vary and most songs are sung at a level where all words are clearly heard (bearing in mind that it is the poetry or words that are important throughout Polynesian music).

The beat is regular throughout a song, though the tempo or speed can vary. Some songs make use of accelerando, speeding up as the song progresses. Other songs vary the tempo of each verse, alternating between fast and slow. Slowing down at the conclusion of a song is also a frequent device.

Traditional Fijian group singing is comprised of many layers of sound and, with up to eight independent parts, the effect is polyphonic. Each of the levels of sound has its own style and role within a composition and is given a name. The five most important and frequent are the:

- *Laga*: literally means 'to sing'. The *laga* begins the song.
- *Tagica*: means 'to cry' or to 'chime in' and it enters at a higher pitch than the *laga*.
- *Druka*: the lowest line, sung by the chorus.
- *Vakasalavoavoa*: a descant line (the highest line), frequently sung in a falsetto.
- *Vaqiqivatu*: the intermittent voice, or occasional brief entry of a voice.

♪ Listening

Listen to 'Ni Sa Bula', a song of welcome, on the tape. It is a song based on Western harmony and melodic line. How many voice parts can you hear? Are there any accompanying instruments? Are these traditional or Western?

◁ A conch shell 'trumpet'

A sitting dance with hand gestures

There are groups of songs in Fiji which accompany various activities. For example, songs can be performed for entertainment (e.g. children's songs), or to work by (such as rowing a canoe or cutting down a tree), or they can be part of formal and ceremonial occasions, such as funerals and the *kava* ceremony. (The *kava* ceremony is the ritualised preparation and sharing of a slightly intoxicating drink made from the roots of the *kava* plant.) Some *meke* (songs and dances) now performed as entertainment (e.g. for tourists) originally had other purposes, including the fast and vigorous spear and club dances in preparation for war. Dances are generally classified as either sitting or standing.

Traditional Fijian instruments fall into two main categories: idiophones and aerophones. Clapping, usually with cupped hands (*cobo*) or beating wooden stamping tubes (*derva*) provides the most usual rhythmic accompaniment, and there are several kinds of slit drums (*lali*). Because the sound carries long distances, these were originally used for communication or announcing events. They were played in pairs. Smaller *lali* (75–100 cm long) were used to accompany dancing. One person held the drum while another hit it.

Flutes of various kinds, including nose flutes and panpipes, were common melodic instruments. The *davui* or conch shell 'trumpet', made from a triton shell, was the most important ceremonial instrument.

With the coming of the missionaries to the Pacific, simple Western harmonies, rhythms and hymn tunes were adopted, in part because of their basic similarity to the traditional music: the use of call-and-response, group performance, and the four-part singing of church music has identifiable similarities with the layered texture of Fijian song.

'Isa Lei' is a popular song using Western tonal structure and harmonies:

Isa Lei

Fijian Farewell Song
Transcribed by G. H.

Is - a Is - a vu - la - qi la - sa di - na_____ No - mu
Ca - va be - ka ko a mai ca - ka va_____ No - mu

la - ko, au na ra - ra - wa ki - na
la - ko, au na se - qa ni

la - sa_____ Is - a le - i Is - a le - i Na no - qu ranu - ma (Bau na - nu - ma) Na no-da jou

ra - wa (na no-qu-ra ra-wa) Ni ko sa na (ni ko sa na) Vo - do e na
la - sa (na no-da jou la - sa)

ma ta - ka_____ Bau na - la - sa ma - i

su - va na - nu - ma ti - ko ga.

Questions
1. What is the main instrument in Fijian music?
2. What are the two main categories of Fijian instruments?
3. What are the layers of sound used in traditional songs?
4. The two styles of dance are called . . .?
5. Describe the melodic style of Fijian songs.

Maori Music of New Zealand

The Maori are the New Zealand natives of Polynesian origin. The Maori migrated to New Zealand from Tonga in the Polynesian Islands between the 10th and 14th centuries, and developed a strong cultural and social community until the arrival of the Europeans around the middle of the 19th century. The Maori population currently numbers around 250 000 out of a total New Zealand population of more than four million.

Maori music is of two types: the traditional Maori chant, and the more recent action song which began in the 20th century and is based on popular tunes.

The Maori chant has many similarities to the traditional music from Polynesia and meets similar social and ceremonial needs. Chants can be classified into categories according to the function they have to fulfil in the society, as well as the way they are performed: either sung or recited.

Chants are performed without any breaks (in a continuous style) and the rhythms are additive, which means that successive notes in a rhythm get progressively longer rather than divisive (progressively shorter).

Recited songs, or chants, have no stable pitch organisation and are performed at a rapid tempo. They are generally performed socially, by groups of singers in unison, and are led by a person whose job it is to choose the starting pitch, and set the tempo. Many chants, especially those of strong social significance, must be performed without change or mistake as errors in performance are considered bad omens. Because of this, many traditional songs have remained unaltered over many generations.

◁ A *haka*   △ Maori women perform a *poi* dance.

There are several categories of recited songs including:

- *Karakia*: chanted spells, ranging from childish charms to chants for more important social events such as the blessing of houses and canoes, to powerful rites and rituals performed by priests. They are chanted in a rapid monotone which is punctuated by long sustained notes. The notes at the ends of phrases are marked by descending slurs or glissandi. The *karakia* must be performed word-perfect or it is believed severe punishment, such as death or disaster, will occur. *Karakia* are often performed by two priests who attempt to create a long, unbroken vocal sound.

- *Haka*: shouted dances with accompanying actions. Originally they had many uses: as entertainment, to welcome visitors to a village and as war dances used before a battle. This latter tradition is maintained today as *hakas* are often performed before body contact sports such as football matches. *Hakas* were originally performed by both men and women but today they are mostly sung by men. The *haka* is a form of ritualised shouting between a solo leader and the responding chorus. The tempo is slow and the song is accompanied by a stylised dance made up of stamping; large, defined gestures of the arms; quivering hand movements; and various facial distortions such as poking out the tongue, wide open eyes and grimacing. The overall effect is one of stylised and controlled aggression, giving away its war-like origins.

Listening
Listen to 'The Gun Haka' on the tape. Notice the inflections of the solo voice and the descending glides at the ends of phrases. The words of the solo are rapid, contrasting with the group response. Body percussion provides occasional accompaniment.

- *Paatere*: songs generally sung by women. The words are based on kinship, heritage and other social values which concern her role in the social hierarchy.

- *Waiata*: sung styles (*waiata* meaning 'song') that are concerned mainly with death and dead kin. They are performed by a group, in unison, at funerals. The melody is repetitive and is not varied. A leader, who can be either male or female, begins the song and performs melismatic solos called *hianga* at the end of each line of text. Others in this category may concern love but usually are about lost love or unhappiness.

- *Pao*: songs about matters of local interest performed for entertainment. The leader begins with a short and improvised solo section. The chorus echoes the solo giving the singer time to think of the next few lines. The melody is freely ornamented but has an overall descending shape and the range is quite narrow.

- *Poi*: dances generally performed by women who swing small balls (*poi*) on the ends of string as an accompaniment to their singing. These songs are quite fast and their range is narrow. Each successive note in a melodic phrase is longer than the preceding one, which means that the rhythm is additive, and the melody is repeated many times to make up the song. The slapping of the *poi* balls on the off-beat creates a rhythmic accompaniment. The *poi* is a group song throughout and does not have solos (*hiangas*).

- *Oriori*: often described as lullabies, these were originally stories and legends which told the history of the tribe. This tradition of reinforcing the kin history is found throughout the music of Polynesia. The words of *oriori* are performed in a continuous stream and the tempos are fast. The soloist often begins or ends a section.

'Pokare Kare Ana' is a famous Maori love song. Though using Western melodic structure, traces of traditional song structure are seen by the use of intermittent harmony line and in the additive rhythm — the final notes of each phrase being longer than the previous ones.

Pokare Kare Ana

Traditional Maori Love Song
Transcribed by G. H.

Po - ka-re Ka-re A - na   Nga wai-o Ro-to-ru - a

Whi-ti a-tu koe-e hi - ne   Ma-ri-no a-na e

E hi-ne e   Ho ki mai ra

Ka ma-te ah-au   i te ar-oh - a e.

Of all the races of Polynesian descent, the Maori has the least number and variety of instruments. As with the Australian Aboriginals, chordophones (strings) and membranophones (drums) are not used in the music of the Maori. There are a number of idiophones, however. The Maori instrument most resembling a drum is the *pahuu*. Instruments with similar names are found throughout Polynesia e.g. the *pahu* in Tahiti and *pa'u'* in the Cook Islands. However, these instruments are real drums made with a shark skin head. The Maori *pahuu* is a wooden gong made from a flat slab of wood about 1.5 metres or longer. The slab often has a depression or hole cut in the centre and is suspended. It was used originally as a warning signal against attack rather than as a musical instrument.

The *kooauau*, a Maori flute played at an oblique angle

A *haka*. Notice the leader's exaggerated movements and facial expressions

Other percussion instruments include:

- *Poi*: small balls attached to lengths of string, used as a percussive, rhythmic instrument in songs bearing their name.
- *Paakuru*: a thin, flat strip of resonant wood 40–50 cm long and 2–5 cm wide. It is held at one end between the teeth and at the other by the left hand. It is tapped by another shorter stick in time to songs (*rangi paakuru*). The sound can be changed by altering the position of the lips around the stick.
- *Rooria*: a jew's-harp (or jaws harp) which depends on mouth resonance to produce the desired sound. It is made of a short piece of supple wood about 10 cm long. One end is held in the mouth or against the teeth and vocal sounds and lip movements alter the sound while it is plucked. It is a solo instrument, used for self-entertainment, or as a courting instrument. Lovers, it is said, could communicate by holding long conversations on the *rooria*!

Wind instruments or aerophones include:

- *Puutaatara* (or *puu moana*): shell trumpet made out of a large triton shell with a wooden mouthpiece inserted into the cut-off end. Like the *pahuu*, this instrument, with its loud single note, was mainly used to assemble the village people or to rally armies against attack.
- *Puukaaea*: a wooden war trumpet, 1–2.5 metres in length. It was made by splitting a branch of mattai tree, hollowing it out and then binding it together again. It had a wooden mouthpiece and a slightly flared bell. Small pegs inside changed the sound slightly and it was used to make warning blasts when the safety of a village was threatened.

- *Kooauau*: a flute about 12–15 cm long, intricately carved and worn as an ornament around the neck. It has three finger-holes and is played obliquely (not vertically or horizontally). The melodies of the *kooauau* are based on scales similar to those used in the lament songs or *waiata*, and it is used as a solo accompaniment to songs.
- *Nguru*: a flute about 8–10 cm long, made of clay, wood or whale's tooth. It has a tooth-shape, with an upturned end. There are two finger holes on top and one or two underneath. It, too, is worn as an ornament and produces a shrill whistle-like sound.
- *Puutoorino*: a longer flute, 30–60 cm, with a harsh, shrill sound.

Other, less important instruments include the bull-roarer or *puururohuu*, and the *koororohuu*, a wooden disc with a length of thin cord through it which produces a whizzing sound and sometimes accompanies songs.

Questions

1. What are the two types of traditional Maori song?
2. Give the names of three chants and the reasons for their performance.
3. What two categories of instruments are not found in traditional Maori music?
4. What is meant by additive rhythm?
5. Briefly describe these instruments: *kooauau, nguru, rooria, poi, paakuru, puutoorino*

A sitting dance with *pois*

Australian Aboriginal Music

It is believed that Aboriginal people came to Australia during the last ice age, more than forty thousand years ago, trekking overland across the land bridges that joined the tip of Australia to Papua New Guinea and South-East Asia. At the end of the ice age the seas rose, isolating the Aboriginals from most external contact until Europeans discovered and settled Australia in the 18th century.

Music is a vitally important aspect of Aboriginal life. It is through music — song and dance — that the Aboriginal learns about how the world was created (the Dreaming), about the environment and how to live in it, about Aboriginal culture and customs, and the supernatural.

Aboriginal ceremonies which combine song and dance are called *corroborees*, which is a corruption of an Aboriginal word *'carib-berie'* used by a now non-existent New South Wales tribe from the Central Coast (near Sydney) in the 18th century. The term meant 'dance'. Early illustrations show that *corroborees* were traditionally danced by men, with painted bodies, who carried shields and weapons. They were accompanied by singers who also provided various rhythms by clapping or beating sticks or boomerangs together. The *didjeridu* was occasionally used as the accompanying instrument.

Other tribes throughout Australia have their own dialect name for the *corroboree* (e.g. *bora* from a northern tribe) and each tribe has its own individual and specific dances, songs, singing style and accompaniments, although research has shown that, in general, the further north the tribe, the more diversity and freedom is displayed in songs and dances.

All the important events in Aboriginal culture and life are celebrated in the *corroboree*: initiations, death and mourning, fertility rites and, most importantly, the 'contact' Aboriginals have with their ancestors and creator spirits in the Dreamtime.

The Dreamtime, or the Dreaming, is the Aboriginal philosophy which explains how the Aboriginal world and its animals were created.

According to the Dreaming, spirit ancestors originally inhabited the Earth and created all the living creatures, plants and the landscape itself. The spirits also gave the Aboriginals the rules for looking after the land and everything that lived in it, and the laws and ceremonies that the Aboriginals had to keep, and rituals that had to be observed. This philosophy was handed down through song, dance, painting and story-telling.

Some of these *corroboree* ceremonies are 'open' for all to see, hear and participate in (including men, women, children and non-Aboriginals) while others are 'closed' — too powerful to be observed or participated in by all but the specially initiated few. Others have parts that are both open and closed.

Corroborees usually commence after sunset and continue through the night. The participants' bodies are painted to represent spirits or animals, or with secret mystical markings known only to the initiated. These markings can be clearly seen in the glow of the fires as they dance. In one way *corroborees* can be looked upon as the music theatre of the indigenous people of Australia.

Musically, a *corroboree* is made up of a series of short songs (some as short as one minute), with each song (according to tribe and area) accompanied by a dance. These dances consist of choreographed, stylised steps and gestures. Within the 'cycle', each song can differ in pitch, range, melodic line, accompaniment and thematic material.

◁ Aboriginal musicians performing with boomerangs.

Ancient Aboriginal rock paintings such as this show the *didjeridu* used to accompany dancing over twenty thousand years ago. (See left of painting)

The songs and dances of the Aboriginal people have been handed down through the generations, not through written symbols but through an oral tradition and imitation of elders. This process begins when tribal members are children and continues as they grow to initiation and beyond. By these means continuity of Aboriginal culture and beliefs has been maintained through the eons.

Aboriginal music is primarily vocal (with only minimal tuned and rhythmic accompaniment). Musical and performance differences occur between tribes and geographical areas, as well as between the songs themselves. There are, however, some basic generalisations that can be made about Aboriginal music.

The melodies are undulatory or wave-like rather than angular — perhaps a musical imitation of Australia's flat landscape — and tend to move downwards by step. The range within a song can vary from as narrow as two notes to greater than an octave, depending on the song and tribe.

Song

Sung by Jimmy Chapman
Bateman's Bay, 1965

Yai gana bi madhai ja dreban ga mari – ri — ed bungarei

wul-a-wa gaunged a bing a wei ja drebrun ga mari - ri – ed bungarei

wul-la-wa guang-ed a bing a-wei ja drebanga mi-ru – ru.

This song is built on two pentatonic scales. The first (up to the rest) is built on the notes:

The second part of the song is built on the notes:

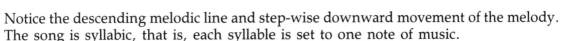

Notice the descending melodic line and step-wise downward movement of the melody. The song is syllabic, that is, each syllable is set to one note of music.

Unlike Western melodies, which are organised around harmonies and scales and so have a feeling of key, Aboriginal chants can have several pitch centres with the melody moving between them in a descending direction.

Melodies are made up of small melodic fragments or cells which are repeated many times. The technical term for this is 'iterative' and notes which are repeated within the song or chant are often ornamented. In performance, songs require good breath control by the performer to extend the melodic material.

The singer frequently slides and slurs one note into the next. The Aboriginal singing style is open-throated and nasal, which allows the sound to carry well when it is performed in the open. Different songs are performed using varying vocal timbres. There is not much variation in dynamics within or between songs and there is no vocal vibrato.

Aboriginal performers with *didjeridu* and clapping sticks

Group singing is generally in unison, although interesting effects can occur if singers vary the rhythm or melody they are singing compared to the other performers in the group.

Aboriginal songs or chants are accompanied by only a few instruments. In central and southern Australia, songs are mainly accompanied by idiophones while songs from the north of Australia generally have more interesting melodies as well as more varied accompaniments, such as the *didjeridu* (the Aboriginals' only pitched instrument) and drums.

Aboriginal songs are classified into several categories according to the way they are performed and their subject matter. These include:

• Children's songs: these perform a role similar to the nursery rhymes that Western children learn. They are basically learning songs which explain the environment and how to live in it. Improvisation is common in these chants.

• Women's songs: because women do not have the number of opportunities to perform that are available to men, there are fewer women's songs. However, their songs perform important social roles to do with mourning, fertility and love-magic. Many are for closed performance only.

• Men's songs: there are a great number and diversity of these and, as with the women's songs, many are for closed performance.

Ceremonial dancers

- Cult songs: these usually have something to do with the Dreamtime, the spirits and ancestors of the Aboriginals, or specific aspects of a tribe's environment such as rocks and waterholes. These songs, and variations of them, can be passed between tribes, with each tribe adapting the story and landmarks to its own specific needs and performance.

- Clan songs: these belong to specific family groups and are handed down from father to son. They are often improvised upon and are important in bonding a particular family group together. For this reason they remain within the tribe. They are considered sacred and are often sung at important rituals such as initiations, circumcisions and funerals.

Listening

Listen to 'Bardainy' ('Hibiscus Rope') on the tape. The piece is performed by two singers, accompanied by clapsticks and *didjeridu*. Notice the drone and its upper harmonic and isometric rhythm.

Many Aboriginal songs and dances, especially those of great importance to the tribe, have been handed down unchanged for thousands of years as the Aboriginals believe that to vary the performance in any way would destroy the strong magic surrounding it.

Musicians prepare for a ceremony with *didjeridu* and clapping sticks

Instruments

Though Aboriginal music is primarily vocal, voices are seldom unaccompanied. Aboriginals use the resources found in their environment to create rhythmic and pitched accompaniments. Handclapping, body slapping and foot stamping are common accompaniments. Other rhythmic instruments include the clapsticks or rhythm sticks which are made of wood. One is usually made of a hardwood and is long and flat. The other is of a lighter wood, shorter and more rounded. When struck together they produce a bright, metallic sound. The rhythm is usually regular and isorhythmic. Boomerangs can be used like rhythm sticks, being clapped together or rattled. Sticks beaten against a shield, a bark bundle or on the ground produce a different sound. Frequently the side of a *didjeridu* is tapped while it is played.

Less common idiophones include rasps (a notched stick scraped by a smaller one), seed-pod rattles (found only in Cape York) and log drums. The bull-roarer, a wooden board swung around on the end of a string makes an eerie sound which represents the supernatural. It is rarely heard except in closed rites which are restricted to initiated men only.

Drums are not found anywhere in Australia, except for a few tribes in Cape York where, through contact with the nearby islands of Melanesia, they were probably introduced. These are of the single headed, hourglass kind with a goanna or lizard skin head.

The *didjeridu*, a wood trumpet, is the instrument most associated with Aboriginal music, but traditionally it was played only in Arnhem Land and the very far north of Australia. It is an aerophone made from a branch or trunk of a Eucalyptus tree that has been hollowed out by termites. It is cut to a length of between one and two metres, then the bark is stripped off and it is smoothed and coated with beeswax. The mouth or blowing end is about 12 cm wide. Sometimes mud or a shell is put in this end to help maintain

A *didjeridu* player

the pressure when blown. The other end is slightly flared. Once made, it is painted with symbolic decoration, and is often kept in a stream to preserve its soft tone.

The *didjeridu* is blown with vibrating lips and the constant rhythmic drone is maintained by the method of circular or continuous breathing. This technique requires the inhaling of air through the nose while at the same time pushing air from the lungs by squeezing the stomach muscles in. The cheeks are used as a reservoir for the air. The pitch varies between instruments according to their size and length.

The sounds produced by the *didjeridu* range from the fundamental note and its harmonic series, up to nine tones in all. Usually, though, there are only two tones produced, a tenth apart. Vocal sounds such as hums, squawks, gurgles and imitations of bird and animal calls can also be made through the *didjeridu*. Rhythmically, the *didjeridu* can produce complicated and changing patterns.

In performance, the rhythm sticks and *didjeridu* usually start and finish first, leaving the voice to finish alone. Though the melodic line of a song may be accompanied by the *didjeridu*, the two are independent of each other.

Questions

1. What is a *corroboree*?
2. Describe a typical Aboriginal song.
3. Describe the Aboriginal singing style.
4. Each of the following songs are performed for a different reason or function. Give the reason: children's songs, women's songs, clan songs, cult songs.
5. What is the most common accompaniment to a song?
6. What aerophone is most associated with Aboriginal music and where is it traditionally found?
7. What sounds and rhythms can the *didjeridu* produce?

Papua New Guinea

The Pacific Ocean contains three main cultural and ethnic areas — Polynesia, a chain of islands scattered north-east from New Zealand to Hawaii; Micronesia, made up of thousands of small, mainly coral islands to the east of the Philippines; and Melanesia, which means literally the 'black islands' found to the north-east of Australia, south of the equator. Indonesia is to the west and Polynesia to the east.

The major island within Melanesia is Papua New Guinea, but other island groups include the Solomons, Vanuatu, New Caledonia and Fiji. The people and languages throughout Melanesia are diverse, though they are thought to have originated in South-East Asia.

Papua New Guinea was originally settled around thirty thousand years ago. Its history has been one of isolation, with only occasional contact with the Malays (Chinese sailors) and then Europeans. Many parts of Papua New Guinea, especially the inland mountainous regions called the Highlands, were left totally isolated from Western contact until the 1960s and 1970s. The music of Papua New Guinea has remained unchanged for most of this time and is believed to be the oldest music in the Pacific.

There are 700 different language groups in Papua New Guinea and a wide variety of musical styles. Traditional music in Papua New Guinea is performed by kin groups or whole communities rather than by individuals, and is functional, which means that it is performed for a particular occasion or purpose.

Music accompanies major life events such as births, initiations, marriages, warfare, fertility rites, feasts and mourning. These events can be ceremonial (such as birth, circumcision and initiation, marriage, farewell and welcome, death and mourning, magic, warfare and peacemaking), or can be social (occasions for enjoyment as in courtship, celebrations and feasts, building a new house or canoe, or the making of a drum). Music also accompanies work — especially if it is rhythmical work where teamwork is required, such as cutting down trees, building houses, or rowing. Specific groups within the population — for example, children, fishermen, old people and men only — have their own special music.

Music in Papua New Guinea today is mainly associated with men, but legend has it that music began with women and that the men stole the ability from them. Many instruments are also said to have been discovered by women although, over time, instrument-making, playing, dancing and singing have become primarily male occupations. Many instruments are made for specific initiation rites and are hidden from women's sight during their making and between performances, as well as being played only out of their hearing.

The traditional occasion for music making in Papua New Guinea is the 'sing sing'. These occasions are both ceremonial and for entertainment. The performing groups sing and dance, usually in exotic costumes of leaves, feathers, masks and make-up. Tapa cloth costumes are made and decorated by men (isolated from women till all preparations are completed); headdresses are elaborate and are made from Bird of Paradise plumes, white cockatoo feathers or other exotic bird plumage. Instruments such as drums are often made for a specific performance and the performers adorn themselves with decorative body art. A 'sing sing' can last as long as twenty-four hours and though performed by the whole tribe, only one man, the leader, will know all the verses, correct costume decoration and dressing and actions of the dance. The leader must dance for the duration of the 'sing sing'.

◁ A *kundu* or hourglass drum

Tribal dancers with drums

With Western contact and influence, traditional songs and dances have undergone many changes. The traditional 'sing sings', for example, have become more urban, social events, with performing groups from many villages travelling considerable distances to take part.

The coming of Christianity also influenced traditional music with hymn tunes now frequently performed. Since the 1920s and 1930s, Western popular music (often sung in pidgin English) has become widespread, with bamboo bands made up of stamping tubes, panpipes, guitar and voices performing folk and other popular music.

Vocal music predominates throughout Papua New Guinea with group singing taking precedence over solo performance, although in performance it is common for one person to lead the singing with the chorus answering in unison or octaves. This style is called responsorial singing.

Songs vary in style and range. Melodies can be made up of as little as two notes (narrow range) or up to an octave or more. A song may consist of one to five phrases, with the lengths of the phrases varying from relatively short to quite long. Melodies are undulating or wave-like and repetitive. Downward movement is gradual and by step; upward movement is by leap. Long notes tend to be at the beginnings or ends of phrases. The repetition of phrases with regular drum ostinatos underneath often creates a hypnotic effect with an almost African sound.

Singing styles make use of slurs between the notes, staccato effects, wailing and falsetto (singing in a falsely high voice). Melodies are not sung to a strict beat and the performer often pauses or can decorate the tune rhythmically with syncopations if desired. Vibrato is absent.

A Highland sing sing

♪Listening

This solo for jew's-harp is from Gizra on the south-west coast of Papua New Guinea. The sound of the jew's-harp imitates the sound of the bull-roarer, which is used during initiation ceremonies.

Songs occupy an important place in a non-literate society. They provide social contact, teach cultural lessons and are a way of transmitting information much like newspapers and books do in Western society. Songs vary in performance style and melody according to their type. A few examples might include:

- Mourning songs: typically sung in a wailing voice. They are only performed by women and can become quite emotional with a wavering in the voice developing as the song progresses. The melody is repetitious and the words describing the dead person are improvised by the wife or mother as she sings.
- Courting songs: these usually have a narrow range (up to an octave) and are sung unaccompanied by men.
- War songs: these are group songs and are performed in a responsorial style, to create the maximum effect.

Traditional music is handed down from generation to generation, with the identity of the author forgotten. With more modern songs, the person who first created them is recognised as the author and it is important that permission is obtained and correct payment made to this person before the songs are performed. Good musicians are highly praised and respected in Papua New Guinea.

Instruments

Instruments in Papua New Guinea are all made from natural materials — wood, bamboo, cane, gourds, shells and animal skins.

The most representative Papua New Guinea instrument is the *kundu* drum. This is an hourglass drum about 750–1050 cm long. It is made of hollowed-out wood with lizard, snake or possum skin stretched over one end to make the head. Pellets of wax are put onto the head to tighten it and alter the pitch, making it higher. *Kundu* drums are usually played while dancing and can be held by a handle attached at the waist. They are considered a man's instrument. Sometimes, in performance, up to three hundred *kundu* drums might be played at the one time to accompany singing and dancing. They all play the same rhythm, maintaining the beat and giving a very African feel to the music. Along the coast of Papua New Guinea, a variation of the *kundu* drum is made in the shape of a fish or crocodile with jaws.

The *kaluli* drum, a single headed drum about 90 cm long, is popular along the southern Highlands. Like the *kundu* drum, only men may make and play them. They are played with a fast and regular beat. Magic is associated with drums and their making, and so they are often made in secret and hidden in the men's huts between playings.

Idiophones (percussion instruments apart from drums) include shell rattles which are worn as ornaments on wrists and ankles when not being played. Rattles made from seed pods are popular accompaniments to dancing, as are gourd rattles containing seeds, and those made of coconut and bamboo. Many of these rattles have names derived from the sound they make: for example, *jileleng*, *baliklik* and *leleleleng*. In some places in Papua New Guinea they are hidden from the women.

Jew's-harps

Bamboo flutes, a conch shell 'trumpet' and drums

Slit drums and slit gongs — made from a hollow log of wood with a cut or slit along the whole upper side and intricately carved and decorated (*garamut*) — are used for signalling or to accompany dancing.

Percussion tubes made of hollow wood or bamboo, and struck by beaters, are sometimes used as a substitute for the slit drum, or when bamboo bands play popular music.

The most widely used wind instrument is the conch shell trumpet, made from a triton shell by boring a hole in the tip. They are played solo or in groups. They are not strictly musical instruments but used for signalling or summoning men for feasts, initiations or other events, though sometimes they are played in ensemble with drums. Conch shells are valuable and are traded throughout Papua New Guinea, so even in the Highlands, far from the coast, many of these instruments can be found.

Several kinds of flutes made of bamboo — both endblown and side-blown — are found throughout Papua New Guinea. Endblown flutes between 45–70 cm long and with a varying number of finger-holes (between two and seven) tend to be recreational instruments. They are not decorated and playing techniques and tunings vary between tribes. Considered young men's instruments, they can be played individually and are often used for enjoyment or courtship. Flute tunes are based on songs which are decorated and improvised upon.

The following tune is a seasonal piece traditionally played during the rainy season. It was transcribed (or copied) from a piece originally played on a bamboo flute. Try to play it on recorder. Notice that there are no bar lines, but there is an underlying regular beat. Can you describe the melody — its shape, range and the number of notes that it uses?

Bamboo Flute Melody

Gizra, Papua New Guinea
Transcribed by P.D.H.

Moderate speed

Side-blown flutes are considered sacred and believed to have supernatural qualities. They are between 30–90 cm long, intricately decorated and traditionally played in pairs. The magic surrounding them is so strong that women and uninitiated males are forbidden to see or touch them. Between playings, they are kept hidden in the men's houses. They are always kept as a pair and if one is damaged, the other must be destroyed. They are used in ceremonies of special significance such as initiations or to summon the spirits.

Bamboo and cane panpipes made of separate tubes of different lengths can produce different notes or sound clusters. They can be played solo or in large panpipe orchestras, producing intricate melodies. They are often used to accompany singing at initiations.

Jew's-harps (mouth harps) are common solo instruments throughout Papua New Guinea, used for individual entertainment or courting. Made of bamboo, they are between 15–20 cm long. By varying the mouth, tongue and jaw positions, many different sounds can be produced, and bird calls, water and other natural sounds imitated. Names given to the jews-harp are onomatopoeic, imitating the sounds it makes — *gongigongo, kongkong* and *bingoro*.

Other instruments include bull-roarers (used in initiations), leaf whistles made from bent leaves and blown for entertainment or on ceremonial occasions, *ocarinas*, and earth drums. String instruments are not common, but there are several examples of one and two-stringed instruments (chordophones).

A side-blown flute

Questions

1. Is Papua New Guinean music considered Asian, Polynesian, Melanesian or European?
2. Papua New Guinean music can be described as functional. What does this mean?
3. Is music in Papua New Guinea generally a communal or an individual activity?
4. Music can be performed for ceremonial or social reasons. Give three occasions that could be considered ceremonial and three that might be social.
5. What is a 'sing sing'?
6. Briefly describe each of these song types, how they sound and who might sing them: mourning songs, courting songs, war songs.
7. Many Papua New Guinean songs are sung in a responsorial style. Describe this method of group singing.
8. What are the two main drums played in Papua New Guinea?
9. Name four representative idiophones found in Papua New Guinea.
10. Which kind of flute would most commonly be played around a Papua New Guinean village — endblown or side-blown? Give reasons for your choice.

Activities

In this section you will find some activities to apply to pieces of music, either the ones included in this book for listening and playing, or ones you choose yourself.

Activity 1: Music Influenced by Traditional Music

Find an example of a piece of music influenced by traditional music, for example, 'Sun Music III' (Sculthorpe), 'Anklung' and 'Goldfish Through Summer Rain' (Boyd), 'Pagodes' (Debussy), 'Pantoum' from *Trio in A Minor* (Ravel), 'Tabuh Tabuhan' (McPhee), 'Choros' (Villa-Lobos), 'Appalachian Spring' (Copland), 'Harry Janos Suite' (Kodaly), 'Lachian Dances' (Janacek), 'African Sanctus' (Fanshawe). After listening to the music, fill in the following.

Title of piece _____

Composer _____

Country of influence _____

Is this the composer's own country? If not, why or how was it chosen?_____

_____

_____

_____

_____

_____

How is the influence shown? (scale, melody, rhythm, form, instruments, text, etc.)

_____

_____

_____

_____

_____

Activity 2: Worksheet for Study of One Piece

Choose a piece of music from a country that interests you, listen and, if possible, perform it. When you know the piece of music, fill in the following.

Title _____

Country _____

Instruments used _____

_____

_____

Scale form

Distinctive rhythms

Form _____

_____

If the music has a specific function, explain it. _____

_____

_____

What musical characteristics of this piece make it typical of its country? _____

_____

_____

_____

_____

_____

_____

Activity 3: Profile of an Instrument

Choose an instrument that interests you, listen to it in performance, find out about it, its background and use, then fill in the following.

Name of instrument _____

Country/countries of use _____

Description (materials, dimensions, method of playing, etc.)_____

_____

_____

_____

_____

Type of instrument (string, wind, percussion, brass)_____

Sachs–Hornbostel classification (see Section 1)_____

Does this instrument have special uses? If so, explain._____

_____

_____

_____

Describe this instrument's history._____

_____

_____

_____

Name the music you listened to as part of this activity._____

_____

_____

_____

_____

Use this space to draw a diagram of the instrument, labelling the parts (strings, reed, etc.).

Activity 4: Another Country

Use this worksheet to help you study the music of other countries not treated in this book. Choose a country to study, listen to and perform the music of that country, then fill in the following.

Country _____

Pieces studied _____

_____

_____

Instruments _____

_____

_____

_____

Scale types

Distinctive rhythms

Forms used _____

_____

_____

Functions of music _____

_____

_____

_____

_____

Activity 5: Transcription

Transcribing what you hear into notation is a very important part of the study of music as it develops your aural skills and can be a way of learning the music and also learning about its use of musical elements such as rhythm, melody, harmony, etc. Use either the staves, or the blank space provided below, to write out some of the music you listen to. (Look at the section on the notation of Chinese music, page 14. This may give you some ideas about how to transcribe music which cannot be notated on the five-line stave.)

Activity 6: The Sachs–Hornbostel System of Instrument Classification

This activity is to help you study the Sachs–Hornbostel system of classifying musical instruments. Before starting it, you should re-read the information on this in Section 1. Remember, this system exists in addition to other means of categorising instruments (such as the most common which divides instruments into string, woodwind, brass, percussion), but is an important method to learn when studying the music of other countries for which these groupings might not be suitable. One reason for their unsuitability is that they imply the division of instruments by reference to Western music and the way we think of it. The Sachs–Hornbostel system, by its scientific nature and its process of using an instrument's nature to classify it, avoids these implications.

1. Define each of the Sachs–Hornbostel categories

• idiophone _____

_____

• membranophone _____

_____

• chordophone _____

_____

• aerophone _____

_____

2. Select one instrument for each grouping. Explain how these instruments fit into their groups.

a. idiophone _____

_____

_____

_____

_____

_____

_____

b. chordophone

_____

_____

_____

_____

_____

c. membranophone

_____

_____

_____

_____

d. aerophone

_____

_____

_____

_____

Answers

Asia

China

1. Formative Period: 3000 BC– 400 AD
   International Period: 400–900 AD
   National Period: 900 –1900 AD
   World Music Period: 1900 AD–
2. Pentatonic or five note scale.
3. There are several different parts or instrumental lines, but all are playing a variation of the melody.
4. *Ya* was virtuous music of the upper and ruling class. *Su* was folk music or music of the peasants.
5. Metal, silk, stone, earth or clay, leather or hide, gourd, bamboo and wood.
6. Where foreign culture, instruments etc. are over time accepted as being Chinese.
7. There are more than three hundred variants of Chinese opera.
8. *Sheng*: male role
   Dan: female role
   Jing: the character with the painted face
   Chou: the clown
9. Clappers, cymbals, drums, *pipa*, fiddles and wind instruments such as flutes and *sona*.
10. *Erhu* (two-stringed fiddle), *qin* (zither), *pipa* (lute), *sho* (a mouth organ), *di* (flute), *chin chin* (three-stringed lute).

Japan

1. China and Korea.
2. *Gagaku* is the traditional classical Japanese music adopted from the Chinese imperial court music.
3. *Kangen*: instrumental
   Bugaku: singing or dancing
4. *Kugaku* is music of the ordinary people, or folk music.
5. All instruments play the same basic melody but each varies the tune slightly (rhythmically or melodically).
6. Pentatonic scale of two types: *yosempo*, for simple melodies
                               insempo, minor sound, for elaborate melodies.
7. *Jo*: quiet passage
   ha: outburst of energy
   kyu: concentration of this energy into a single point of expression.
8. *Noh*: highly formalised music theatre
   Kabuki: melodramatic form of music theatre
   Bunraku: puppet theatre
9. *Taiko*: membranophone; *ryuteki*: aerophone; *sho*: aerophone; *koto*: chordophone; *hichiriki*: aerophone; *biwa*: chordophone.

Korea

1. *A-ak*:   ritual court music of Chinese origin
   Sog-ak: folk music or music of the people
2. court music   religious music

   ```
              \    ┌──────┐        ┌───────┐   /
               >   │ A-ak │ —ak—   │ Sog-ak│  <
              /    └──────┘        └───────┘   \
   ```
   hyang-ak   folk music
   (Korean traditional music)
3. China.
4. Japan.
5. *Komungo*: six-stringed zither, plucked with bamboo rods.
   Kayagum: twelve-stringed zither, plucked by hand.
6. Court dances are generally slow and ritualised; folk dances are faster and more athletic.
7. Speed. Court music is slow, stylised and the syllables of each word are extended. Folk songs tend to be quicker, syncopated and sound more Indian than oriental.
8. Korean indigenous classical music.
9. *Pansori* is a Korean one-man opera or narrative.
10. *Piri*:   bamboo (aerophone)
    ching: metal   (idiophone)
    boo: clay   (idiophone)
    eo: wood   (idiophone)
    pyongyong: stone   (idiophone)
    changgu: skin   (membranophone)
    komungo: silk   (chordophone)

Vietnam

1. a. China.
   b. By the scales and instruments used.
2. Mixture of religion, Chinese influence, regional differences, the rule of the French.
3. Because each region has its own tonal dialect and the melodies of the songs must reflect the rise and fall of speech.
4. a. Pentatonic.
   b. *Nam* (happy) and *bać* (sad).
5. Music played on the *dàn tranh*, usually by girls.
6. Since before the 15th century.
7. a. 1917.
   b. 'Vong Cò'.
8. String: *dàn tranh, dàn nguyet, yang k'in, dàn nhi*, guitar, *dàn ty ba*
   Wind: *sona, kouan, ken*
   Percussion: gongs, drums
9. a. *Dàn*.
   b. *Dàn tranh, dàn nhi, dàn ty ba, dàn nguyet*.
10. That the songs are used in relation to specific events such as weddings, funerals, etc.
11. Pentatonic.
12. *Hoa-la* means 'flowering' and refers to the practice of spontaneous elaboration and improvisation as music is performed. Its result is the distinctive heterophonic sound of Vietnamese music.

Indonesia

1. '*Gamelan*' means an Indonesian ensemble of tuned percussion, the music this group plays, and the idea of music in general.
2. a. Colotomic structure is the method of composition used in the *gamelan*. Each instrument has its own role which fits into the overall melodic and rhythmic structure.
   b. The higher the instrument, the faster its rhythm.
3. *Panerus* (smallest), *barung* (middle), *slentem* (largest).
4. Javanese *gamelans* are more sedate than Balinese, Sundanese use *suling* and *rebab*, Balinese are vibrant and slightly out of tune.
5. a. *Pelog* (seven notes), *slendro* (five notes: pentatonic).
   b. *Patets* have implications of mood and can signify times of the day and night.
6. *Kroncong* is a style of folk music accompanied by plucked string instruments. Portugal.
7. *Dangdut* is named for the sound of drumming and it must contain a drum.
8. European.
9. *Gamelans* accompany dances, shadow puppet plays, puppet plays, and 'operas'.
10. Percussion: gongs, drums, *trompong* (*bonang/kenong*), *kendang*, *cheng cheng*, *jegogan* (*gender*), *saron* (*saron*), *anklung*, *gambang*
    String: *rebab*, *celempung*
    Wind: *suling*

India

1. Ancient chants to the gods.
2. *Ragas* are the scale-melodic basis of Indian music.
3. *Talas*.
4. *Sam* is the first and most important beat of the *tal*.
5. *Alap*: the raga is enunciated and improvised upon (solo)
   Jor: the percussion instrument enters
   Gat: the extended improvisatory section which builds up in excitement to the conclusion.
6. Carnatic: *vina* (melody) and *mridanga* (rhythm)
   Hindustani: *sitar* (melody) and *tabla* (rhythm).
7. The Persian or Moghul Empire had the greatest influence (primarily in the north of India). Many instruments of Persian descent are found in Indian music e.g. *rebab*, *sitar*, *tabla*, *sarengi* and *sarod*.
8. Violin, clarinet and squeezebox.
9. Improvise means to make up as you go along. Indian music is basically a set of variations on a theme — the variations being improvised.
10. *Bansari*: aerophone (flute)
    Mridanga: membranophone (drum)
    Mandira: idiophone (cymbals)
    Pungi: aerophone
    Sahanai: aerophone ('oboe')
    Sarengi: chordophone (four-stringed bowed fiddle)

Eastern Mediterranean

Iran

1. The *tar* and *setar*, the *rabab*. The *sitar*, the *rebab* the guitar, and the *rebec*.
2. Pairs of small kettledrums. The *nakkers*.
3. The call to prayer (*azan*), and learning the Koran by chanting passages from it.
4. A poet/musician who accompanies himself on the *saz*. *Asik* in Turkey and *guslar* in Yugoslavia.
5. The interludes are based on the melody.
6. The traditional classical music of Iran.
7. *Maqam*: the Arabic word that refers to the scale system of *radif*
   Avaz: the Iranian term for the same thing
   Dastgah: scales.
8. *Darb* is the area of rhythm in *radif*. It is learnt through mnemonic syllables.
9. Membranophones: *darabuk*, *def*, *dohol*, *naqqara*.
   Chordophones: *saz*, *tar*, *setar*, *ud*, *kemenche*, *geichek*, *santur*, *qanun*, *rabab*, *tambur*
   Aerophones: *sorna*, *ney*, *ney-arbun*, *karna*.
10. The *sorna* and *dohol*. *Davul-zurna*, *zurle* and *goć*.

Turkey

1. *Türkü*: local secular songŝ
   Sarkï: urban songs
   Bozlak: love songs
   Âgit: mourning songs
   Destan: ballads and narrative songs.
2. The use of extremely high pitch, and the interpolation of ornaments.
3. The phrases start on high notes but end on lower notes, and the phrases have set numbers of syllables, 8, 8, 8, 6.
4. Syllabic: each syllable of the text is set to one note
   Melismatic: a syllable is set to a number of notes.
5. Dervishes are members of a male religious order dating from the 13th century. Dance is used as part of their ceremonies.
6. a. Into four groups, ♩♪ ♩♪ ♩♪ ♩♪ b. This is called *aksak* or 'limping'.
7. *Zurna* and *davul*. The *zurna* is a double reed instrument and the *davul* is a large drum.
8. *Saz* and *baglama* (long-necked lutes), *kaval* and *duduk* (flutes), *kemence* (three-stringed fiddle), *argul* and *tulum* (bagpipes), *keman* (violin), *def*, *deblek*, and *darabak* (drums).
9. Because the music uses scales that include intervals smaller than Western semitones.
10. a. Aeolian, Dorian, Ionian, Mixolydian.
    b. Aeolian starting on 'g'.
11. a. *Uzun hava* are long semi-improvised melodies played by shepherds.
    b. They are based on melodic formulae.
    c. They are played on a *kaval*, a 70 to 100 cm long vertical flute.
12. a. An *asik* is a poet/musician.
    b. The *saz*.

Greece

1. Weddings, funerals, work and religious festivals.
2. *Kleftic* ballads are songs about the *klefts*, Greek fighters who resisted the Turks.
3. *Kleftic* ballads are about historical events or the lives of the *klefts*.
4. This song only has a range of one octave.
5. a. 7/8 and 5/8
   b. *Kalamatianos*, 3 + 2 + 2,
6. *Klarino*:   clarinet   (aerophone)
   Flogera: flute   (aerophone)
   Lauto: lute   (chordophone)
   Santuri: dulcimer   (chordophone)
   Gaida: bagpipe   (aerophone)
   Mandolino: mandoline   (chordophone)
   Bouzouki: type of lute   (chordophone)
7. The *bouzouki*.
8. *Rembetika* is a type of music, a mixture of Turkish and Greek music created by the arrival of Turkish refugees in Greece from the mid 19th century until the Second World War.
9. '*Aman*' is used melismatically as the chorus of many rembetic songs.
10. The *baglamas*.
11. The *hassapiko* is a line dance; the *zembekiko* is a solo dance.

Yugoslavia

1. Singing in harmony.
2. The first has the parts close together; the second uses consecutive thirds.
3. a. *Kolo* means 'around'.
   b. A *kolo* is a dance.
   c. It is danced by a group, not pairs.
4. a. Time signatures with 5, 7, 9, 11 beats in a bar.
   b. 'Bolen Leži Mlad Stojan', the Macedonian dance tune, the Macedonian wedding song.
   c. Both were in 7/8.
5. The use of changing time signatures.
6. a. A *guslar* is a singer of historical epics.
   b. The *gusle*.
   c. A one-stringed fiddle.
7. *Guslar* music is not notated, it is learnt 'by ear' from another *guslar*.
8. Bowed: *gusle*, *lirica*
   Lute type: *tanbura*, *saz*
   Dulcimer type: *kanun*
9. a. *Tarabuka*: goblet shaped with a single head
      Def: large single-headed frame drum
      Goć: bass drum.
   b. *Goć*.
10. a. A *sazet* is a village instrumental ensemble.
    b. The word is derived from the Turkish word '*saz*', which means 'instrument'.

Africa

The Music of Africa

1. To accompany activities, for religious rituals, as a link between life and culture.
2. War songs, planting songs, lullabies, songs for minding cattle, music for weddings and other ceremonies.
3. *Griots* are musicians who are believed to have contact with the spirit world through music. They sing about history, legends, accrued wisdom, proverbs and poetry. Senegal and the West Africa area.
4. Some African languages are tonal and, because of the way some drums are constructed and played, the pitches and rhythms of the languages can be transferred to drumming.
5. To accompany singing, dancing, and rituals, as a symbol of royalty, for sending messages, for poetry recitation, as a means of preserving tribal history and knowledge, representing a god.
6. The simultaneous use of different meters.
7. It is palindromic.
8. Pentatonic: the music is based on only five notes
   Call-and-response: a musical device in which a solo performer alternates with a group or chorus, the soloist usually has different phrases while the group answers with the same phrase all the time.
9. *Balophon*:   idiophone (xylophone)
   Kora: chordophone (harp-lute)
   Kalengu: membranophone (drum)
   Jenjili: chordophone (fiddle)
   Sanza: idiophone (gourd resonator with tuned keys attached)
   Inanga: chordophone (zither).
10. Call-and-response, repetition with minor variations, handclapping as accompaniment.
11. It is pentatonic, it has complex rhythmic interplay and syncopation, it uses solo–group singing, and has repetition.

South America and the Caribbean

South America

1. Because South America is made up of thirteen countries with different cultures.
2. Andean music and the music of Brazil.
3. a. In the Andean regions.
   b. In Brazil.
4. a. Drums, flutes, conch shell 'trumpets', rattles.
   b. Drums, panpipes, *ocarinas*.
5. The players use complicated rhythms that fit together and sound as if one person is playing.
6. *Charango*:   small, high pitched guitar made from an armadillo shell
   Cuatro: small four-stringed guitar
   Tiple   three-stringed guitar
   Guitarrone: large four-stringed guitar.
7. A *quena* is an Andean flute made from the legbone of a llama.

8. A *bombo* is an Andean bass drum. Its skin is unshaven, resulting in a dull sound, and it is often played with two different rhythms at the same time.

9. a. South American Indians, Portuguese, Africans.
   b. South American Indians: flutes and various percussion instruments, links between singing and dancing.
   Portuguese: the use of European harmonies and melodies, the popularity of string instruments, the use of rhythmic ambiguity between 6/8 and 3/4.
   African: importance of rhythm and dance, use of drums and percussion, playing on 'non-musical' instruments, polyrhythm and syncopation, instruments such as the *berimba*.

10. Polyrhythm and syncopation.

11. a. *Maxixe*, *merengue*, *samba*.
    b. *Samba*.

12. A modern *choro* is a piece of instrumental music that is typically Brazilian.

13. Strings: *charango*, *cuatro*, *tiple*, *guitarrone*, *cavaquinho*, harp, violin, *berimba*
    Winds: flutes, panpipes, *ocarinas*, *quena*
    Percussion: drums, rattles, *bombo*, *congas*, *afoxe*, *chocalho*, *agogo*, *reco-reco*, *maracas*, *claves*, *cabasa*
    Other: conch shell 'trumpet'.

The Caribbean

1. a. Guitars, banjo, *berimba*, *claves*, *maracas*, *cabasa*, *reco-reco*, *agogo*, *congas*, *bongos*, bottles hit with spoons, frying pans, saucepan lids, boxes, petrol drums, *quinto*, bamboo and wooden flutes.
   b. Percussion.

2. The use of stringed instruments, simple European harmony.

3. In the names of instruments (*aprinting*, *abeng*), in musical terms (*mambo*, *kumina*), in dance steps, religious ceremonies, and dance rhythms.

4. a. *Mento* is the folk music of Jamaica.
   b. Offbeat guitar accompaniment, prominent bass line, improvised melodic line around a tune.

5. The use of simple chords, the use of repetitive chord patterns.

6. Call-and-response, pentatony.

7. a. *Kromanti* and *kumina* are the music rituals of descendants of African slaves.
   b. In the use of African words and phrases, the names of instruments, the rhythms used, and performance style.

8. a. Calypso is a song type from Trinidad.
   b. Satirical, humorous.

9. a. The top is cut off a petrol drum and the lid is then beaten to make different notes.
   b. Ping-pong, guitar, cello, bass.
   c. Brake-drum hubs.

10. a.
    b. Syncopation.

11. Their rhythms.

12. The use of simple harmony, and the use of chordal ostinato.

The Pacific Region

Polynesian Music

1. Tonga was the first and Hawaii, the last.
2. The words or the text.
3. Style: the way it is performed.
   Function: why and for what purpose it is performed.
4. Narrow range, uses only a few notes, and part-singing.
5. a. *Ula*.
   b. Accelerating tempo, melody made up of short repeated phrases, uses only a few notes in the melody, accompanied by percussion instruments.
6. Acculturation is when aspects of one culture are adopted by another culture and they become indistinguishable. In music, the use of Western chordal and melodic structure and instruments by non-Western cultures.
7. a. *Mele hula* is a sung dance of Hawaii.
   b. Hawaii emphasises individual performance while Tonga emphasises group performance.
8. *Fasi* and *laulalo* are parts in Tongan group songs. *Fasi* is the melody line, *laulalo* is the drone bass.
9. *Tarava* is Tongan gospel singing.
10. *Uliuli*:   seed pod rattle (idiophone)
    Pahu: sharkskin headed drum (membranophone)
    Fangufangu: nose flute (aerophone)
    Ukelele: banjo (chordophone).

Fiji

1. The voice.
2. Aerophones: blown instruments, such as flutes.
   Idiophones: clapping, slit drums, etc.
3. *Laga*:   first voice
   Tagica: second vocal entry
   Druka: lowest melodic line, the chorus
   Vakasalavoavoa: descant line
   Vaqiqivatu: a voice which enters occasionally.
4. Sitting and standing dances.
5. Melodies have narrow vocal range, made up of one to four note scales, melodies descend at ends of phrases, slow down at end of songs.

Maori Music of New Zealand

1. Chants and action songs (recited or sung).
2. *Karakia*: chanted spells, blessings and religious rituals
   Baka: dances of welcome, or for entertainment or war
   Paatere: women's songs.

3. There are no strings (chordophones) or drums (membranophones).
4. Additive rhythm is where each note in a phrase is longer than the previous one.
5. *Kooauau*:   flute
   Nguru: whale's tooth-shaped flute
   Rooria: jew's-harp
   Poi: twine balls on ends of string
   Paakuru: mouth bow
   Puutoorino: flute.

Australian Aboriginal Music

1. *Corroborees* are Aboriginal song and dance ceremonies.
2. Songs are short in overall length, melodies are made up of short, repeated cells and have a narrow range, melodies tend to move downward, by step, smoothly.
3. Singing style has a nasal quality, slides and slurs between notes of the melody, no vibrato, no changes in dynamics.
4. Children's songs: learn about the environment
   Women's songs: social role, e.g. mourning, love-magic, fertility
   Cult songs: songs about the Dreamtime
   Clan songs: songs about the tribe.
5. Handclapping, rhythm sticks.
6. The *didjeridu*, found in Arnhem Land and far north Australia.
7. A low drone and notes of the harmonic series, plus other vocal sounds, hums, animal cries, etc.

Papua New Guinea

1. Melanesian.
2. Functional means that music making occurs for a reason or to fit a particular purpose or occasion.
3. Communal.
4. Ceremonial reasons include births, deaths, circumcision and initiations, marriage, farewell and welcome, death and mourning, magic, warfare and peacemaking. Social reasons might be feasts and celebrations, building a new house, completing the making of a canoe or a drum.
5. Sing sings are ceremonial and social get-togethers for the communal making of music.
6. Mourning songs: sung by women in a wailing, emotional voice. The melody is repetitious, and the words improvised
   Courting songs: narrow range, sung unaccompanied by men
   War songs: sung by men in a responsorial style.
7. Responsorial style is similar to call-and-response, i.e. one person sings a solo, and is answered by the chorus.
8. *Kundu* and *kaluli* drums.
9. Four idiophones might include the jew's-harp, slit drum or gongs, rattles of various kinds and bamboo percussion tubes.
10. Endblown flutes would more often be played around a village as the side-blown flutes are considered sacred and are kept hidden from sight (except for sacred initiations and rites) because of the strong magic that surrounds them.

Lyric Translations (Literal)

Hua Ku Ko
(The Flower Drum)

Feng-yang drum, feng-yang gong,
Let's sing and play the drum and gong.
What song will we sing?
We only know one song, the feng-yang
    song,
Feng-yang, the flower-drum song.

Drr-lang-dang-p'iao-yi-p'iao, (repeat)
Drr-p'iao, drr-p'iao,
Drr-p'iao-drr-p'iao-p'iao yu
Drr-p'iao-p'iao-p'iao-p'iao-yi-p'iao.

(She) I am sad and unhappy,
I married the flower-drum player.
He is stupid. All he does is play his drum.

Drr-lang-dang, etc. . . .

(He) I am sad and unhappy,
I married an ugly woman.
She has the biggest feet you ever saw.

Drr-lang-dang, etc. . . .

Haralambis

Come, friend Haralambis,
So that we can marry you off,
So that we can eat and drink
And dance.

Refrain:
I don't want her!
You must take her!
Talk to me about something else, my friends.
What behaviour is this,
Forcing a man to marry!

Dispense with these words
And with these wails.
Old Haralambis
Does not want to marry.

Think well, Haralambis,
And speak more logically,
And I will persuade you
To put on the wedding band.

Kato Stou Valtou Ta
Horia
(Down in the Village of
Valtou)

Down in the village of Valtou,
Xiromeron and Agrafa,
And in the five districts,
Eat, drink, my brothers.

Wherever there are many klefts
Ornamented with gold,
They sit and eat and drink,
While terror spreads in Arta.

They write a letter
Insulting the beard of the Kadi,
They also write to Komboti,
They worship the bishop.

Consider it well:
We will burn your villages.
Quickly the armatoli
Will come like wolves.

Ryotsu Jinku

If the Rankan bridge in Ryotsu fell down,
I would still continue my journey.
On the river the men are collecting
    cuttlefish.

Why aren't you here?
Is it because the wind is not strong enough?
Or don't you have a cargo?
Or do you have to stay in Niigata?

I hear the plovers.
All night I must watch from the lighthouse,
And see the stars.

Are you thinking of me?
How could I not think of you
As I cross the valleys?

Arirang

Arirang, Arirang, Arariyo.
Arirang, the road is long.
If you leave me, my love,
You'll be lame before you've walked three
  miles.

Cò Lả
(The Egret Flies)

The egret flies without tiredness,
From the market town gate
To the countryside.
It makes me remember . . .

Kouh Beh Kouh
(On the Road)

Along the side of the mountain,
Wild reindeer were running.
My loved one was there too,
And this made me very happy.
Hoi! Hoi! Hoi!
My lovely Hadjar,
So happy and lovely.

Along the side of the mountain,
I hunted a racing rabbit,
My loved one was there,
Wearing a gold earring,
Wearing a gold earring,
Hoi! Hoi! Hoi!
My lovely Hadjar,
So happy and lovely.

Apo Ti Porta Sou Perno
(I Pass By Your Door)

I pass by your door
And find it locked.
Alas, alas, beautiful May.

I stoop to kiss the lock,
Pretending to kiss you.
Alas, alas, beautiful May.

Hát Hôi Trăng Răm
(Song of the Full Moon)

Let's climb high up the hill,
Sit beneath the banyan tree,
Sit and sing under the tree.
If you love me, climb with me,
To sit beneath the tree.
The moon is full for us to see,
The moon is full for us to see.

Isa Lei

Isa, Isa, you are my love,
If you leave me I will be lonely,
Like the flowers miss the sun at daybreak,
I'll always miss you.

Isa Lei, night is coming,
Tomorrow I will be sad.
Don't forget me when you are
Away from Suva Bay.

Bibliography

Bartok, B., *Turkish Folk Music from Asia Minor*, Princeton University Press, Princeton, 1976

Bebey, F., *African Music: A People's Art*, Harrap, London, 1969

Bellhouse, A., *Asian Music for Beginners*, William Brooks, Sydney, nd

Berliner, P., *The Sound of Mbira*, University of California Press, Los Angeles, 1981

Craig, D., *The Chinese Orchestra: An Alternative Instrumental Group for Schools*, Global Music, Hill End, Queensland, 1984

Dao, T., *Essays on Vietnamese Music*, Foreign Languages Publishing, Hanoi, 1984

Ellis, C., *Aboriginal Music: Education for Living*, University of Queensland Press, St Lucia, 1985

Haydon, G. and Marks, D. (eds), *Repercussions: A Celebration of African–American Music*, Century, London, 1985

Hill, M. and Barlow, A. (eds), *Black Australia*, AIAS Humanities Press, New Jersey, 1978

Hollestelle, K., *Music of New Guinea*, unpublished, BMusEd Thesis, New South Wales State Conservatorium of Music, nd

Holroyde, P., *Indian Music*, George Allen and Unwin, London, 1972

Holst, G., *Road to Rembetika*, Anglo-Hellenic Publishing, Athens, 1975

Hood, M., *The Ethnomusicologist*, McGraw-Hill, New York, 1971

Isaacs, J. (ed.), *Australian Aboriginal Music*, Aboriginal Artists Agency, Sydney, 1979

Kassler, J. and Stubbington, J. (eds), *Problems and Solutions: Occasional Essays in Musicology Presented to Alice Moyle*, Hale and Iremonger, Sydney, 1984

Kunst, J., *Music in New Guinea*, Martinus Njihoff, 'S-Gravenhage, 1967

Lai, T. and Mok, R., *Jade Flute: The Story of Chinese Music*, Shocken Books, New York, 1985

Liang, D., *The Chinese Ch'in: Its History and Music*, DMY Liang, San Francisco, 1969

Lord, A., *The Singer of Tales*, Harvard University Press, Cambridge, Massachusetts, 1960

Malm, W., *Japanese Music and Musical Instruments*, Tuttle and Co., Rutland, Vermont, 1959

—— *Music Cultures of the Pacific, the Near East and Asia*, Prentice-Hall, Englewood Cliffs, New Jersey, 1967

May, E. (ed.), *Musics of Many Cultures*, University of California Press, Los Angeles, 1980

McPhee, C., *Music in Bali*, Yale University Press, New Haven, 1966

Nettl, B., *Folk and Traditional Music of the Western Continents*, Prentice-Hall, Englewood Cliffs, New Jersey, 1965

—— *Theory and Method in Ethnomusicology*, Macmillan, New York, 1964

New South Wales Department of Education, *Aboriginal Arts in Transition*, Wagga Wagga, 1988

Roberts, J., *Black Music of Two Worlds*, Morrow and Co., New York, 1974

Sargent, B., 'A fly on the Wall: A Lesson in Indian Music at a Middle School', in *Music Teacher*, 68:11, 1989

Vulliamy, G. and Lee, E., *Rock, Pop, and Ethnic Music in Schools*, Routledge and Kegan Paul, London, 1981

Music and Transcription Sources

China

'Hua Ku Ko' from C. Haywood, *Folk Songs of the World*, Arthur Barker Ltd., London, 1966.

'Song of Happiness' from Dale A. Craig, *The Chinese Orchestra: An Alternative Instrumental Group for Schools*, Global Music, Hill End, Queensland, 1984.

Excerpt from 'The River Flowing', *Yang Chin and Er Wu Concerto*, Melody Record Co., Kowloon, Hong Kong.

Japan

Excerpt from 'Naga Uta', *Echigojishi*, UNESCO and Barenreiter Records, London, England.

Excerpt from 'Chidori', *Classical Japanese Koto Music*, Everest Records, Los Angeles, USA.

Korea

Excerpt from 'Kyung Bok Kung Tharyung', *Korean Folk Song Festival*, Hit Record Co., Seoul, Korea.

Vietnam

Excerpt from 'Medley of Three Songs', *Traditional Music of Vietnam*, Lyrichord Records, New York, USA.

Indonesia

'Baris Bapan' transcribed from *The Exotic Sounds of Bali*, CBS Odyssey Records.

Excerpt from 'Selir', *The Exotic Sounds of Bali*, CBS Odyssey Records.

Excerpt from 'Gamelan Piece', *Java: Music of Mystical Enchantment*, Lyrichord Records, New York, USA.

India

Excerpt from 'Ragu Maru — Behag', *Sitar Music: Meditations and Music for Pleasure*, EMI Records, London, England.

'Rag Arrangement' from B. Sargent, 'A Fly on the Wall: A Lesson in Indian Music at a Middle School', *Music Teacher*, 68:11, 1989.

Iran

Excerpt from 'Love Song', *Folk Music of Iran*, Lyrichord Records, New York, USA.

'Kouh Beh Kouh' from C. Haywood, *Folk Songs of the World*, Arthur Barker Ltd., London, 1966.

Excerpt from *Radif: The Traditional Music of Iran*, World Record Club, Victoria, Australia.

Turkey

Excerpt from 'Koylu Dugun Havasi', *Folk Music of Turkey*, Topic Records, London, England.

Greece

'Kato Stou Valtou Ta Horia', 'Haralambis' and 'Apo Ti Porta Sou Perno' from S. & T. Alevizos, *Folk Songs of Greece*, Oak Publications, Embassy Music Corporation, New York, USA.

Excerpt from 'O Travihtos', *Folk Music of the Dodecanese Islands*, Albatros Records.

Yugoslavia

Excerpt from 'E Moj Te Djelen Qi Ne Saba' (Wedding Song), *Yugoslavie: Sous les Peupliers de Bilisht*, Radio France, Paris, France.

Africa

'Sovu Dance' from C. Haywood, *Folk Songs of the World*, Arthur Barker Ltd., London, 1966.

Excerpt from 'Drumming from Rwanda', *An Anthology of African Music: Rwanda*, UNESCO and Barenreiter Records, London, England.

Excerpt from 'Duet for Agidigbo', *Nigeria: Music of the Yoruba People*, Lyrichord Records, New York, USA.

'Rwanda Wedding Song' transcribed from *An Anthology of African Music: Rwanda*, UNESCO and Barenreiter Records, London, England.

'Tu Tu Le Tu' transcribed from *Sounds of West Africa*, Lyrichord Records, New York, USA.

South America

'Yaku Kantu' transcribed from *Musical Atlas: Bolivia*, EMI Records, London, England.

'Zamponeando' transcribed from *Music of the Incas*, World Record Club, Victoria, Australia.

Excerpt from 'Totoras', *Music of the Incas*, World Record Club, Victoria, Australia.

The Caribbean

'Linstead Market' transcribed from *Roots of Reggae: Music from Jamaica*, Lyrichord Records, New York, USA.

Excerpt from 'Oh Carolina', *Roots of Reggae: Music from Jamaica*, Lyrichord Records, New York, USA.

Excerpt from 'Mandumbe', *Jamaican Ritual Music from the Mountains to the Coast*, Lyrichord Records, New York, USA.

'Somebody Whisper to Me' transcribed from *Le Steel Band de la Trinidad: Magie Caraibe*, Arion Records.

Polynesia

Excerpts from 'Sasa' and 'Lamagaffe' from *Festival Music from Western Samoa*, Kiwi Pacific Records, Wellington, New Zealand.

Fiji

Excerpt from 'Ni Sa Bula', *Treasure Island Meke*, Viking Sevenseas Records, Wellington, New Zealand.

'Isa Lei' transcribed from *Treasure Island Meke*, Viking Sevenseas Records, Wellington, New Zealand.

Maori Music of New Zealand

Excerpt from 'Gun Haka', *Haka and Song*, South Pacific Recordings, Plimmerton, New Zealand.

Australian Aboriginal Music

Song sung by Jimmy Chapman, Bateman's Bay, 1965 from *Aboriginal Arts in Transition*, New South Wales Department of Education, Wagga Wagga, 1988.

Excerpt from 'Bardainy' (Hibiscus Rope), *The Morning Star*, Australian Institute of Aboriginal Studies and EMI Records, Australia.

Papua New Guinea

Excerpt from 'Solo for Jew's Harp', *Traditional Music of Papua New Guinea*, Lyrichord Records, New York, USA.

'Flute Melody' transcribed from *Traditional Music of Papua New Guinea*, Lyrichord Records, New York, USA.

Glossary/Index

A

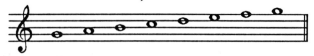

N

O

P

*As Western instruments are referred to throughout the book primarily as a means of classification and description, only major page references to these instruments are given in the index.

Acknowledgments

The authors and publisher would like to thank the following for permission to include copyright material or for assistance with photographs:

Music

CBS Records; Disco-Center Classic, Kassel; EMI Records Australia; Everest Records; Global Music Co.; International Music of Italy; Kiwi-Pacific Records; Lyrichord Records; Melody Record Company; Oak Publications; Radio France; Rhinegold Publishing; South Pacific Recordings; Topic Records.

Photographs

The Academy of Turkish Music and Fine Arts pp. 74, 75, 76; Agence Hoa Qui p. 102; Alexander Turnbull Library pp. 160, 164, 165; Emmanuel Angelicas pp. 74, 75, 76; Bishop Museum, Honolulu pp. 152, 154; Anne Bolt p. 138; Embassy of Brazil p. 122; Michael Calnan, World Expeditions, Sydney, cover photograph; Consulate-General of the People's Republic of China pp. 4, 10, 12, 16, 17, 18, 19; Luis Cuadros, Panorama Tours, back cover photograph, pp. 114, 115, 117, 120; Disco-Center Classic, Kassel pp. 22, 26, 99, 104, 106; Fiji Visitors' Bureau p. 158; Garuda Indonesia, cover photograph, pp. 49, 51; Philip George p. 82; David Gray p. 111; Hamlyn p. 121, 142; Horizons de France pp. 6, 96, 97, 110, 111; John and Penny Hubley p. 128; Indian Tourist Bureau pp. 54, 57, 58, 59, 61; International Cultural Corporation of Australia p. 168; Internationales Institut fur Vergleichende Musikstudien und Dokumentation pp. 36, 38, 40, 43; Jamaica Tourist Board p. 131; Japan Information and Culture Centre p. 24; Korea National Classical Music Institute pp. 33, 34; Korea National Tourism Organisation, cover photograph, pp. 30, 32; Richard Meek p. 78; Michael Friedman Publishing pp. 123, 124; Tony and Marion Morris p. 7; Musee de l'Homme p. 107; National Publishing Station, Wellington p. 161; Pacific Friend Magazine (Jiji Gaho Sha, Inc.) pp. 27, 29; Papua New Guinea Consulate pp. 176, 177, 179; Proteus Publishing Ltd p. 133; Radio France p. 67; Leonie Roser p. 82; RTB p. 92; Stvarnost pp. 88, 92; Blazenko Tomasic; Tonga Visitors' Bureau pp. 148, 150, 151; Topham Picture Source p. 134; Topic Records p. 70; University Museum of Archaeology and Ethnology, Cambridge p. 156; University of California Press: Paul Berliner, *Soul of Mbira: Music and Traditions of the Shona People of Zimbabwe*, photos 14 and 19. Copyright © 1978 The Regents of the University of California p. 103; US Travel and Tourism Administration p. 155; VEB Deutsche Verlag fur Musik p. 5; Weldon Trannies pp. 167, 170 (photograph: John Halfhide), 171 (photograph: Leo Meier), 172, 173 (photograph: Brian Alexander); Yale University Press: Colin McPhee, *Music in Bali*. Copyright © 1966 Yale University Press pp. 44, 48, 49; Vinka Zuvela.

Every effort has been made to trace and obtain copyright. If any infringements have occurred the publisher is willing to make suitable arrangements with copyright holders.